Excavations at the Mycenaean Cemetery at Aigion – 1967

Rescue Excavations by the late Ephor of Antiquities, E. Mastrokostas

Thanasis I. Papadopoulos

Evangelia Papadopoulou-Chrysikopoulou

Archaeopress Publishing Ltd
Gordon House
276 Banbury Road
Oxford OX2 7ED

www.archaeopress.com

ISBN 978 1 78491 618 3
ISBN 978 1 78491 619 0 (e-Pdf)

© Archaeopress and T I Papadopoulos and E Papadopoulou-Chrysikopoulou 2017

All rights reserved. No part of this book may be reproduced, or transmitted, in any form or by any means, electronic, mechanical, photocopying or otherwise, without the prior written permission of the copyright owners.

Printed in England by Oxuniprint, Oxford

This book is available direct from Archaeopress or from our website www.archaeopress.com

In memoriam
of the late Ephor E. Mastrokostas and our beloved wife and mother Litsa

CONTENTS

PREFACE AND ACKNOWLEDGMENTS v
INTRODUCTION 1
THE TOMBS AND THEIR CONTENTS 5
CATALOGUE – DESCRIPTION OF FINDS 7
    TOMB A 7
    TOMB B 13
    TOMB C (3) 16
    TOMB D (4) 23
    UNPROVENANCED TOMB 35
    Pottery sherds with no inventory numbers 38
COMMENTARY ON THE FINDS 41
    I. The Mycenaean pottery 41
    A. Closed Shapes 41
        2. Piriform jar 43
        3. Rounded alabastron 44
        4. Square-sided alabastron 44
        5. Amphoriskos 45
        6. Globular Jug 46
        7. Lekythos 47
        8. Askos 47
    B. Open Shapes 48
        9. Krater (?) 48
        10. Stemmed bowl (?) 48
        11. Kylix 49
        12. Shallow cup 50
        13. Spouted deep cup 50
        14. Throne model 51
    C. Other finds 51
GENERAL COMMENTS AND CONCLUSIONS 53
ABBREVIATIONS 55
    I. For Periodicals and Series 55
    II. Special Abbreviations 55
    III. Descriptive terms used in the catalogue of finds 57
BIBLIOGRAPHY 59
PLATES AND FIGURES 61

List of Plates and Figures

Topographical plan of the Gymnasion at Aigion. vi
Plate I. Map of Mycenaean Achaea (after Giannopoulos 2008) 2
Plate II. Aigion:1967. Representative types of vases. 3
Plate III. Aigion: 1970 excavation of Mycenaean cemetery. 4

Plate 1. Stirrup jars Nos. 414, 415. 61
Plate 2. Stirrup jars Nos. 417, 445, 446, 447. 62
Plate 3. Stirrup jars Nos. 483, 484. 63
Plate 4. Stirrup jars Nos. 485, 486; rounded alabstron No. 487. 64
Plate 5. Stirrup jar No. 548; straight-sided alabastron No. 550; kylix No. 396. 65
Plate 6. Piriform jar No. 397; throne No. 386; stirrup jar No. 387. 66
Plate 7. Stirrup jar No. 569; jug No. 493; jug No. 495; sherds of a large jar No. 496; lekythos No. 387. ... 67
Plate 8. Baseless askos No. 383; rounded alabastron No. 384; stirrup jar No. 385; stirrup jar No. 389. 68
Plate 9. Stirrup jars Nos. 390, 391; jug No. 392. 69
Plate 10. Square sided alabastra Nos. 393, 394; jug No. 475; amphoriskos No. 476. 70
Plate 11. Stirrup jars Nos. 477, 479; jug No. 478. 71
Plate 12. Stirrup jars Nos. 480, 399, 400; amphoriskos No. 398. 72
Plate 13. Rounded alabastron No. 401; straight-sided alabastron No. 402; kylix No. 418. ... 73
Plate 14. Amphoriskoi Nos. 419, 420, 421; straight-sided alabastron No. 422 74
Plate 15. Jug No. 425; amphoriskos No. 426; straight-sided alabaston No. 427, based straight-sided alabastron No. 428. 75
Plate 16. Based askos No. 429; stirrup jars Nos. 430, 431 76
Plate 17. Stirrup jar No. 432; amphoriskoi Nos. 433, 434. 77
Plate 18. Amphoriskos No. 435; stirrup jars Nos. 436, 437. 78
Plate 19. Stirrup jars Nos. 438, 439, 440, 441. 79
Plate 20. Stirrup jar No. 443; based askos No. 488. 80
Plate 21. Stirrup jar No. 489; rounded alabastra Nos. 444, 552. 81
Plate 22. Shallow cup No. 553; kylix No. 564; stirrup jar No. 565. 82
Plate 23. Stirrup jars Nos. 566, 567, 568. 83
Plate 24. Pottery sherds Nos. 100, 104, 110, 101, 102. 84
Plate 25. Pottery sherds Nos. 103, 106, 107, 108, 109, 111. 85
Plate 26. Artefacts. 86

Figure 1. Stirrup jars Nos. 414, 415. 87

Figure 2. Stirrup jars Nos. 417, 445. 88

Figure 3. Stirrup jars Nos. 446, 447. 89

Figure 4. Stirrup jars Nos. 483,484. 90

Figure 5. Stirrup jars Nos. 485, 486. 91

Figure 6. Stirrup jar No. 443; piriform jar No. 397. 92

Figure 7. Rounded alabastron No. 487; throne No. 386. 93

Figure 8. Stirrup jars Nos. 391, 387. 94

Figure 9. Lekythos No. 493; jug No. 392; stirrup jar No. 385. 95

Figure 10. Lekythos No. 382; jug No. 495 96

Figure 11. Baseless askos No. 383; rounded alabastron 384. 97

Figure 12. Stirrup jars/jugs Nos. 479, 389. 98

Figure 13. Jugs Nos. 475, 478; amphoriskos No. 476. 99

Figure 14. Stirrup jars Nos. 480, 399. 100

Figure 15. Amphoriskos No. 398; stirrup jar No. 400. 101

Figure 16. Straight sided alabastron No. 402; rounded alabastron No. 401. 102

Figure 17. Kylix 418, straight sided alabastron 422 103

Figure 18. Amphoriskoi Nos. 419, 420, 421. 104

Figure 19. Jug No. 425; amphoriskos No. 426. 105

Figure 20. Straight sided alabastra Nos. 427, 428; based askos No. 429. 106

Figure 21. Stirrup jars Nos. 431, 430. 107

Figure 22. Stirrup jar No. 432; amphoriskos No. 433. 108

Figure 23. Amphoriskoi Nos. 434, 435. 109

Figure 24. Stirrup jars Nos. 436, 437. 110

Figure 25. Stirrup jars Nos. 438, 439. 111

Figure 26. Stirrup jars Nos. 440, 441. 112

Figure 27. Stirrup jar 569, rounded alabastron No. 444. 113

Figure 28. Based askos 488, rounded alabastron 552, shallow cup 553 114

Figure 29. Stirrup jar No. 489. 115

Figure 30. Carinated kylix 564, stirrup jars 565,566 116

Figure 31. Stirrup jars Nos. 567, 568, 100 (?). 117

Figure 32. Sherds of large piriform jars Nos. 101, 102, 103. 118

Figure 33. Kylikes Nos. 104, 105. 119

Figure 34. Fragments of kylix No. 106, bowl or shallow cup No. 107 and bowl or spouted cup No. 108. ... 120

Figure 35. Fragments of large piriform jars Nos. 109, 110, and pictorial vase No. 111. 121

Figure 36. Artefacts. 122

PREFACE AND ACKNOWLEDGMENTS

Papadopoulos in his work *Excavation at Aigion - 1970* (SIMA XLVI, 1976, VII), referring to the Mycenaean cemetery of Aigion and the four chamber tombs excavated in 1967 by the late Ephor E. Mastrokostas, wrote that 'it is to be hoped that he (Mastrokostas) will soon be able to publish their contents'. Unfortunately, due to his death, this publication never appeared and permission to publish was granted to the excavator of the same cemetery (1970) Prof. Papadopoulos in 1999. Publication of this monograph, therefore, has been delayed not only due to the death of Mastrokostas, but for several other reasons, such as the search for the original excavation diary (never found), checking the preliminary reports, searching for and identifying the finds in the museums of the local Ephorate (Aigion and Patras) and additionally, of course, the work of cataloguing, photographing and drawing the objects.

For permission to publish this material we should like to thank the Local Council of Monuments of Southwestern Greece, and the Ephors of ΣΤ' Ephorate, Dr L. Kolonas and Z. Aslamatzidou, as well as Dr L. Parlama, former Director of Antiquities of the Ministry of Culture. Thanks are also due to archaeologist S. Oikonomidis for drawing the finds and superintendent L. Michalopoulou for help at the Aigion Museum. The photographs of the finds were taken by E. Mastrokostas, J. Sarakinis and Prof. Th. Papadopoulos. We are grateful to Dr D. Davison and Archaeopress for their valuable help in undertaking the final editing, layout and publication of the monograph in the Archaeopress series. Finally, we would like to warmly thank INSTAP for its subvention to cover some of the costs of this publication.

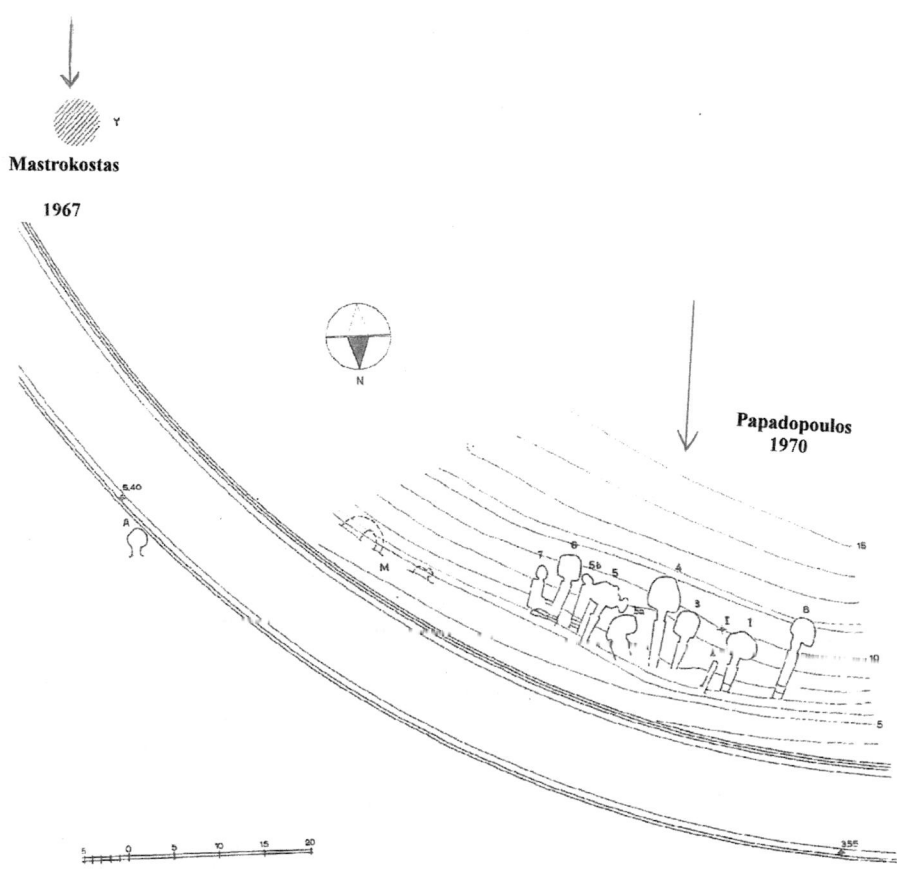

TOPOGRAPHICAL PLAN OF THE GYMNASION AT AIGION.

INTRODUCTION

The modern town of Aigion (Col. Pls. I-II Fig.1a) in NE Achaea, a high bluff controlling the coast road and the fertile plains to the east and west, occupies the site of the ancient city. To the west and southwest rise the slopes of mounts Panachaicon and Chelmos that separate it from central Achaea, while on the opposite coast of the Corinthian Gulf can be seen the mountainous shores of Locris, Phocis and Boeotia, as far up as the Isthmus. The soil is well-watered and fertile, but all the coast has always been subject to earthquakes. The small but interesting port and the natural amenities, combined with the defensible hill, fertile plain and rivers on either side were certainly the original reasons for the settlement on this spot. Aigion is mentioned by Homer (*Iliad* 2.574) as having supplied ships for the Trojan war and being under the authority of Agamemnon.

Aigion was inhabited continuously from the Neolithic to the end of the Late Bronze Age (NL- YE IIIC Late). This is demonstrated by NL sherds discovered in disturbed levels in the town, as well as more numerous EH sherds. From the MH period onwards archaeological remains occur in greater quantities and exhibit a wider variety and are generally more important. These include a LH II megaron-like building, abundant pottery of the LH IIIΛ and LII IIIB-early LH IIIC, and a small number of LH IIIC Late sherds.[1]

The existence of a Mycenaean cemetery west of the town, at the locality of Psila Alonia, below the Gymnasion (High School), was already known before WW II, as evidenced by the short report of Ephor Kyparissis.[2] Ephor Yalouris in 1954 collected some Late Mycenaean sherds from the 15 tombs destroyed and plundered since Roman times.[3]

During work on the new national road from Aigion to Patras in 1967 more chamber tombs from this Mycenaean cemetery were accidentally revealed. Ephor Mastrokostas examined some of them (the actual number of which and their contents are not recorded) in his very brief report in *ADelt* 22, 1967 Chr. 1 and *AAA* 1: 2, 1968, 137 ('απεκαλύφθησαν Υστεροελλαδικοί τάφοι, τινές των οποίων κατεστράφησαν').

In 1970 Papadopoulos conducted systematic excavations at the cemetery (Topographical plan and plate 1a) and examined 11 chamber tombs, the

---

[1] Papazoglou-Mnioudaki, 1998, 85-91; Paschalidis, 2014, 11.
[2] *PAE.* 1939, 104.
[3] *PAE,* 1954, 289f.

contents of which were published in 1976 in a monograph (*Excavation at Aigion - 1970*) in the Swedish series *SIMA* (Vol. XLVI).

After Mastrokostas' death permission to publish his finds was granted to Prof. Thanasis Papadopoulos.

At present 15 (?) chamber tombs have been excavated, but the possibility that the actual number may be far greater cannot be excluded, taking into account those mentioned by Kyparissis and Yialouris. Furthermore the area to the east and south is covered by pine-trees, making it now almost impossible to undertake further investigations of the Mycenaean cemetery.

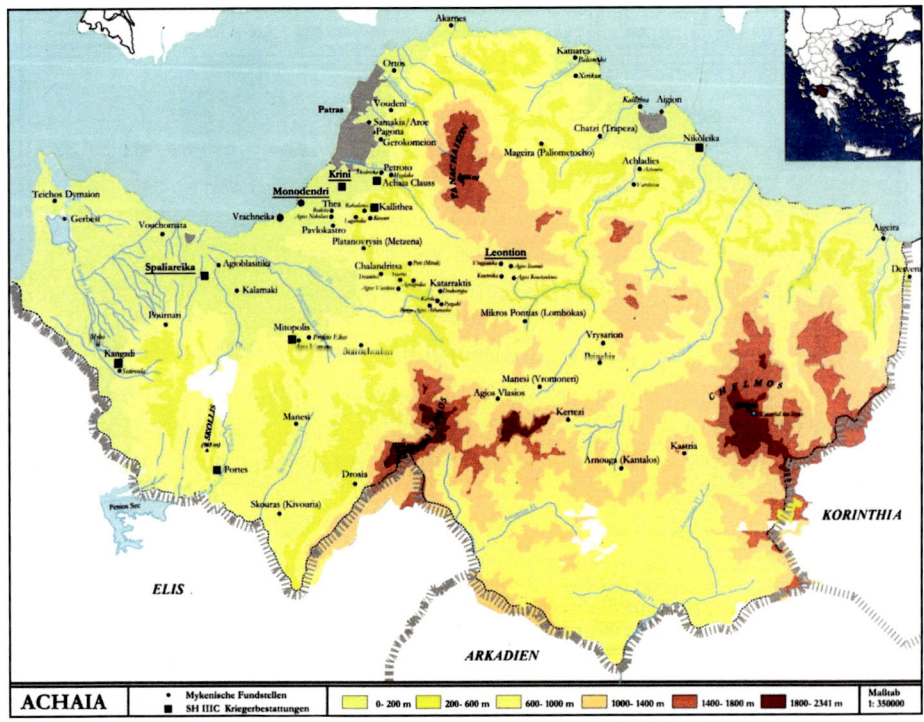

PLATE I. MAP OF MYCENAEAN ACHAEA (AFTER GIANNOPOULOS 2008).

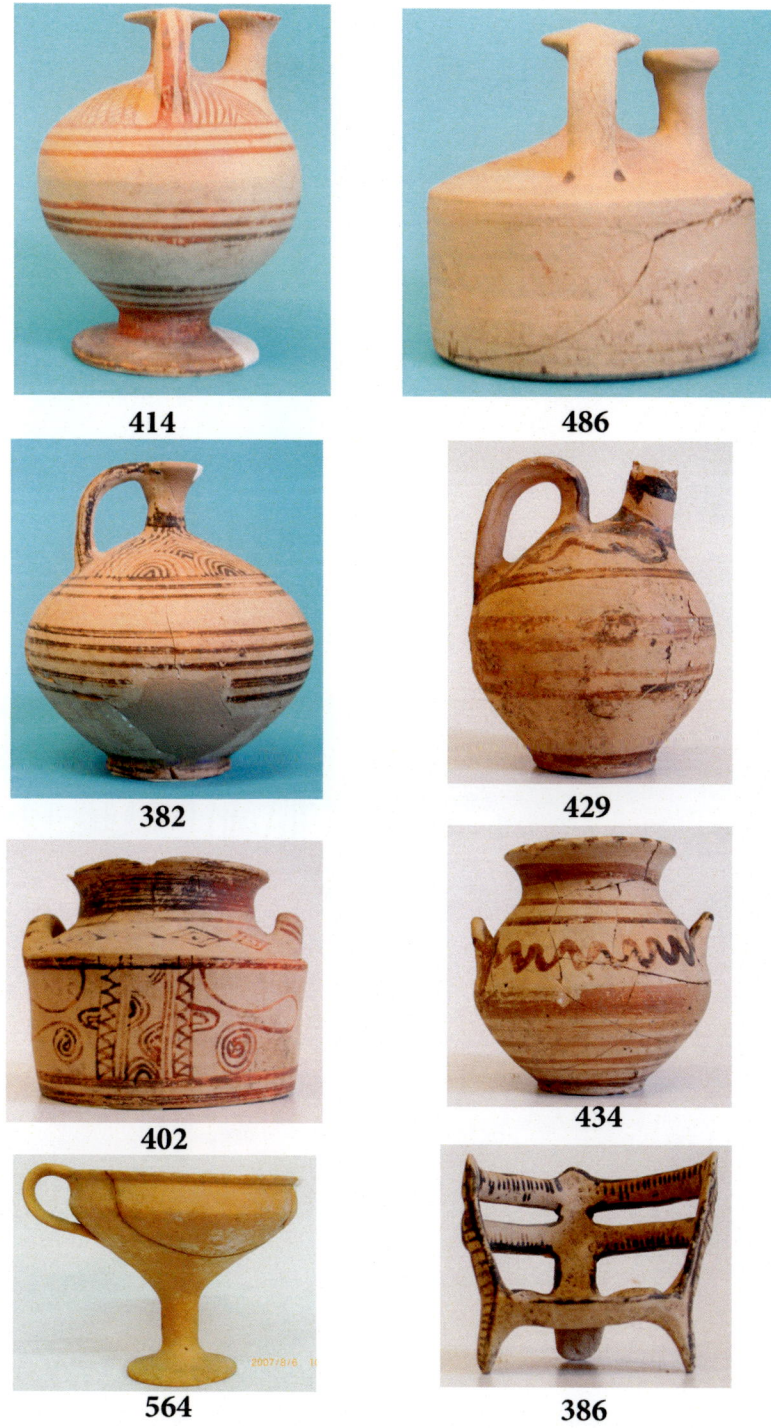

PLATE II. AIGION:1967. REPRESENTATIVE TYPES OF VASES.

PLATE III. AIGION: 1970 EXCAVATION OF MYCENAEAN CEMETERY.

THE TOMBS AND THEIR CONTENTS

During the systematic excavations at Aigion in 1970, Papadopoulos was able to include only four tombs excavated by Mastrokostas, and this number was confirmed by local *phylakas* Michael Papadopoulos, who helped Mastrokostas in his rescue excavations. Thus the entries in the inventory register of the Aigion museum, where the finds have been ascribed to seven tombs (Α, Β, Γ, 1, 2, 3, 4), needed to be corrected and we decided to consider tombs Α, Β, Γ as corresponding to tombs 1, 2, 3. In order to distinguish the four tombs excavated by Mastrokostas in 1967 from those excavated by Papadopoulos in 1970, we shall refer to Mastrokostas' tombs by the letters A, B, C, D (rather than 1, 2, 3, 4). Although scant traces of the tombs excavated in 1967 survive, it is highly possible that they were similar to those systematically investigated in 1970. They lie to the east of them and were cut into the hard rock at roughly the same level.

In contrast to the 11 tombs excavated by Papadopoulos, the four tombs excavated in 1967 produced a much greater number of finds, most probably indicating richer burials.

Since there is no information in Mastrokostas' excavation report on the architecture, stratigraphy and burial customs of those tombs,[1] the finds will be selectively presented according to their typology and fabric. Each item is allocated a double numeral, i.e. a serial number plus the inventory number of the Aigion museum.

---

[1] With the exception of a brief mention in the excavator's report regarding the chronology and the presence of open rectangular pits or cists cut into the floor of some tombs ('οι αρχαιότεροι τάφοι χρονολογούνται εις την ΥΕΙΙΒ-ΙΙΙΑ εποχήν. Εντός τινών εξ αυτών είναι ανοιγμένοι λακκοειδείς τάφοι (ορθογώνια ορύγματα)'.

CATALOGUE – DESCRIPTION OF FINDS

TOMB A

1-414. Piriform stirrup jar. Fig. 1a, Pl 1a.

H. 0.117m; D. 0.09m.
Parts of spout and base lost, otherwise complete and intact. Pinkish clay, pale yellow slip, reddish-brown paint slightly worn off. Globular-piriform body; pedestal foot. The disc of the false neck is higher than the spout. Handles round in section, flat top disc. Paint on lip of spout, inside and out; encircling loop around base of spout and false-neck; spiral on flat top disc; handles decorated with edging lines with their central part left blank. Three groups of bands on body, base painted solid; shoulder zone decorated with two pairs of successive triangles and triangles filled with diaper net.
FS 167; FM 61A; 1, 5.
Cf. French, *BSA* 62 (1967) 152, fig. 2 (Mycenae 52-261), Mountjoy, *MDP*, fig, 127: 1; idem, *RMDP*, figs. 33: 248; 115: 81 (Nichoria), 198: 221 (Vourvatsi), 414: 86 (Rhodes).
LH IIIB1.

2-415. Globular stirrup jar. Fig. 1b, Pl. 1b

H. 0.166m; D. 0.162m.
Small parts of the body, the false neck and one handle are lost, but repaired; otherwise complete and intact. Clay buff-brown, creamy-white slip, black paint mostly worn off. Paint on lip of spout, inside and out; encircling loop around the base of spout and false neck; concentric circles with central dot on flat top disc; handles painted solid except for a small reserved triangle next to the top disc; handle zone decorated with triangles filled with diaper net and elaborate triangle; lower on the upper shoulder, between two groups of double bands, triangles filled with diaper net and concentric semicircles with their interior painted solid. Two groups of bands on lower body, low ring base painted solid.
FS 175; FM 61A: 5; 71: g; 43: b.
Cf. Mountjoy, *RMDP*, fig. 432: 213.
LH IIIC Early-Middle.

3-416. Three clay biconical buttons. Fig. 36, Pl. 26a

H. 0.021, 0.024, 0.031m; D. 0.025, 0.024, 0.034m.
Two (a-b) are complete, the third (c) broken, repaired and 1/3 lost. Dark-brown clay, polished. Undecorated.
Cf. Furumark, *CMP*, 89, fig. 2: 2. For a detailed discussion and references, see Papadopoulos, *Mycenaean Achaea*, 146-47 and notes 37-47.
LH I-II.

4-417. Globular stirrup jar. Fig. 2a Pl 2a

H. 0.221m; D. 0.235m.
Complete except for some parts of the handles, spout, false neck and shoulder, which are lost and repaired. Pale-yellow clay and slip, red-brown paint, partly worn off. Large globular body, straight spout, strap handles, low ring base. Spiral on the slightly concave top disc, lip of spout painted inside and out, encircling loop around the base of spout and false neck; thick edging lines on handles with their central part left blank. Elaborate triangles and foliate band (?) on handle zone; lower on the upper shoulder, between two groups of double bands, alternating simple and elaborate triangles, another group of three bands on lower body; base painted solid.
FS 175; FM 71: g; 25: 11.
Cf. examples listed by Furumark, *MP III*, pl. 99.
LH IIIC Middle.

5-404. Four steatite 'shanked' buttons. Fig. 36, Pl. 16b

Ranging in H. from 0.015m to 0.016m, and in D. from 0.019m to 0.021m. All intact save for minor scratches and chips.
One of black and three of pale green steatite, and all are of Furumark's 'shanked' type (*CMP*, 89, fig. 2c).
See references for No. 3-416.

6-405. Two steatite and one clay buttons. Fig. 36, Pl. 16c

Ranging in H. from 0.010m to 0.019m, and in D. from 0.013 to 0.019m. The steatite conical specimens (one purple the other black) are intact, half of the clay biconical one is missing. Parallel vertical incisions on the surface of the purple button.
See references for Nos. 3-416 and 5-404.
LH III.

7-406. Glass seed-shaped bead, ribbed vertically. Fig. 36, Pl. 16d

L. 0.012m; D. 0.006m.
Cf. Papadopoulos, *Mycenaean Achaea*, figs. 287, 325: 10.
LH III.

8-407. Ring of gold wire, well-preserved, undecorated. Fig. 36, Pl. 16e

D. 0.027m.
Simple gold rings are known from several sites.
Cf. Higgins, *GRJ*, 83, Iakovvidis, *Perati B*, 294 and Papadopoulos, *op. cit.* for discussion of the shape and use of the several types of Bronze Age rings.
LH III.

9-408 Two bronze fragments. Fig.36, Pl. 16f

They belong to an arm of a pair of depilatory tweezers. Badly corroded.
Pres. L. 0.032m; 0.015m.
Cf. Iakovidis *op. cit.* 284-85 and Papadopoulos, *op. cit.* 148-9 for discussion and references.
LH III.

10-445. Globular stirrup jar. Fig. 2b, Pl. 2b

H. 0.012m; D. 0.93m. Complete.
Red-buff clay and slip, black semi-lustrous paint almost entirely worn. Concave spout with splaying rim; flat top disc, low ring base.
Base painted solid, spiral on top disc, rings around base and rim of spout and false neck; horizontal bars on outside of handles; two groups of bands on body; shoulder zone decorated with triangles and circles with cross fill.
FS 171; FM 61A: 6; 17: 28.
Cf. Mountjoy, *MDP*, figs. 93, 128; *RMDP*, fig. 37: 278 (amphora).
LH IIIA2-B.

11-446. Globular stirrup jar. Fig. 3a, Pl. 2c

H. 0.0126m; D. 0.117m.
Broken, but largely complete except for the spout.
Pinkish-buff clay and slip, red-brown paint entirely worn off.
Low ring base, slightly convex top disc with small central elevation.
Base painted solid, spiral on top disc, encircling loop around base of spout and false neck; horizontal bars on the backs of handles; groups of bands on body, groups of vertical lines on body zone; upper shoulder decorated with multiple

triangle framed by groups of oblique lines in the semicircle and oblique chevrons on the quadrants.
FS 173; FM 61A: 1; 58: 7; 64: 22.
Cf. Mountjoy, *op. cit.* fig. 129: 1; idem, *RMDP*, figs. 259: 159 (Tanagra), 415: 90 (Rhodes).
LH IIIB1.

12-447. Globular stirrup jar. Fig. 3b, Pl. 2d

H. 0.136m; D. 0.133m.
Complete except for the upper half of the spout.
Red-buff clay and slip, black semi-lustrous paint mostly worn off.
Low ring base, flat top disc. Base painted solid, handles decorated with edging lines, separate rings around the base of spout and false neck, concentric circles with central dot on top disc. Lower undecorated; groups of broad bands and fine lines on upper body to line of spout attachment; upper shoulder decorated with concentric semicircles.
FS 173; FM 43: d.
Cf. Mountjoy, *MDP*, fig. 154: 4.
LH IIIB2/C Early.

13-483. Piriform stirrup jar. Fig. 4a, Pl. 3a-b

H.0.129m; D. 0.092m.
Body broken and restored, small fragments missing.
Buff clay and slip, dark-brown paint partly worn off.
Torus disc base, flat top disc. Bands around the base, stem monochrome, belly zone decorated with vertical wavy lines; a group of wide bands on upper body below handles, connected isolated semicircles on the shoulder semicircle, double semicircles on the quadrants; concentric circles on top disc, rings around the rim and base of spout and false neck, edging lines on handles.
FS 167; FM 53: 33-34; 43: 32, e.
See references for No. 1 BE 414.
LH IIIB1-2.

14-484. Globular stirrup jar. Fig. 4b, Pl. 3c-d

H. 0.135m; D. 0.12m.
Body broken and restored, small fragments missing.
Reddish-buff clay and slip, brown paint partly worn off.
Ring base, slightly convex top disc with small central elevation.

Base painted solid, groups of bands and fine lines on body; narrow belly zone decorated with simple zig-zag pattern; flowers on the upper shoulder zone; rings around rim and base of spout and false neck; concentric circles with central dot on top disc, simple vertical line on handles.
FS 173; FM 61: 2; 18: 128.
Cf. examples listed by Furumark, *MP. III*, pl. 98, no. 173: 2 (Aigina) Mountjoy, *MDP*, fig. 129; idem, *RMDP*, figs. 33: 250 (Mycenae), 115: 82 (Messenia) 134: 59 (Olympia) 145: 44 (Achaea), 198: 226 (Attica), Papadopoulos, *Aigion*, fig. 58b.
LH IIIB1.

15- 485. Conical stirrup jar. Fig.5a, Pl. 4a-b

H. 0.106m; D. 0.127m.
Restored from many places, most parts of the handles, false neck and a large part of body missing.
Light-brown clay, buff slip, red-brown paint partly worn off.
Torus base and outside of handles painted solid. Group of wide bands on lower body, two groups of wide bands and fine lines on upper body, flowers on upper shoulder; rings around rim and base of spout and false neck.
FS 182; FM 18: 136.
Cf. examples listed by Furumark, *op. cit.* pl. 105; Mountjoy, *MDP*, fig. 131; idem, *RMDP*, figs. 34: 255 (Prosymna), 70: 131 (Zygouries), 134: 60 (Elis), 199: 229-231; Papadopoulos, *Mycenaean Achaea,* figs. 117 f-I, 118 a-c.
LH IIIIB1.

16-486. Cylindrical stirrup jar. Fig. 5b, Pl. 4c

H. 0.102m; D. 0.103m.
Broken and restored, small parts missing.
Buff clay and slip, dark-brown to black paint, almost entirely worn off.
Concentric circles on the slightly convex with centrally elevated top disc; wide wavy band on handles, ring around rim spout, encircling loop around the base of spout and false neck. Cylindrical body decorated with wide bands and concentric semicircles; chain of three lozenges on the semicircle of the shoulder, triangles with diaper net and solid interior on the quadrants.
FS 184; FM 43: 13, 73: (?)
Cf examples listed by Furumark, *MP III*, pl. 106; Giannopoulos 2008, pls. 65, 67: 6-7 (Leontion, LH IIIC (?)); Benzi, *RCM*, pl. 153: I (Rhodes); Kanta 1980, figs. 14: 4, 44: 7, 49: 2 (LMIIIA-C, Crete); Morricone, *Annuario* 43-44 (1965-66), fig. 333 a-b (Kos-Langada).
LH IIIB2.

17-487. Rounded alabastron. Fig. 7a, Pl. 4d

H. 0.082m; D. 0.104m.
Broken and restored, small fragments missing.
Pinkish-buff clay and slip, dark-brown paint partly worn off.
Concave neck with sloping lip; baggy body; two horizontal round handles; round base. Neck painted solid inside and out; two broad bands below handles, another around base of neck, below which parallel vertical lines; underneath the base three concentric circles.
FS 85; FM 72: 13.
Cf. examples listed by Furumark, *op. cit.*, pl. 50; Mountjoy, *RMDP*, fig. 341: 92 (Thessaly).
LH IIIB-C.

18-548. Globular stirrup jar. Pl. 5a

H. 0.0197m; D. 0.0182m.
Broken, restored, complete.
Pinkish clay, buff slip, dark-brown paint, slightly worn off.
Ring base painted solid. Alternating semicircles with solid interior on the belly zone between two groups of bands. Dotted joining semicircles and triangles (?) on shoulder.
FS 176; FM 43: b, 27; 42: 21 (?)
Cf. Benzi, *RCM*, pls. 24H, 107 g-h, l; Mountjoy, *RMDP*, fig. 430: 196-198, 200 (Ialysos-Rhodes).
LH IIIC Early.

19-549. Globular jug.

H. 0.0153m; D. 0.0134m.
Complete. Reddish clay, light-brown paint. Globular baggy shape, short narrow neck; flat vertical handle; ring base. Two groups of bands round the neck and lower body (?)
FS 114.
LH IIIA2.

20-550. Straight-sided alabastron. Pl. 5b

H. 0.073m; D. 0.064m.
Complete. Pink clay, yellow-buff slip, red paint, partly worn off.
Narrow concave neck with flat horizontal rim; angular shoulder and cylindrical body tapering slightly towards flat base; two loop handles set horizontally on shoulder. Neck painted solid inside and out; handles barred; handle zone

decorated with a horizontal chain of lozenges; rest of body banded; concentric circles underneath base (?).
FS 96; FM 73: 3.
Cf. Benzi, *RNC*, pl. 94m; Mountjoy, *RMDP*, figs. 121: 123 (Messenia), 147: 70 (Achaea) 344: 115 (Pteleon) 425: 165 (Ialysos-Rhodes).
LH IIIC Early.

21-551. Steatite button. Fig. 36, Pl. 16g

H. 0.014m; D. 0.017m.
Intact. Greyish steatite, polished. Conical shape, with bevelled edge.
Furumark, *CMP*, 89, fig. 2: 1a.
LH III.

TOMB B

22-396. High-stemmed kylix. Pl. 5c

H. 0.142m; D. rim 0.136m.
Complete, restored from many pieces. Pinkish clay, yellow slip, red paint almost entirely worn off. Relatively deep rounded bowl with narrow everted rim; high narrow stem slightly tapering downwards. Flat disc base hollowed by a small cavity corresponding to diameter of stem. Two vertical flattened handles rising slightly above rim and extending from rim to just below the shoulder. Monochrome.
FS 265.
Cf. Papadopoulos, *Aigion,* pls. 27, 35: BE. 637; *Attica,* fig. 10: F1-F2; Blegen, *PN 1.2*, pl. 363, shape 29g.
LH IIIA2 Late.

23-397. Piriform jar. Fig. 6b, Pl. 6a

H. 0.169m; D. body 0.135m; rim 0.097m.
Broken, restored, complete. Surface one side much abraded. Pinkish clay, yellow-buff slip, dark-brown to black paint, partly worn off. Piriform shape; wide concave neck with sloping lip; three vertical strap handles; torus foot, the underside is slightly concave. Solid paint on neck and mouth, inside and out; handles painted solid; Diaper net on shoulder framed by thin bands above and below; fine and broad bands on lower body; foot painted solid, the underside is reserved.
FS 31; FM 57: 2.
Cf. examples listed by Furumark, *MP III*, pl. 22; Mountjoy, *RMDP*, fig. 20: 104 (Argolid).
LH IIIA1.

24-386. Throne. Fig. 7b, Pl. 6b

H. 0.06m; D. 0.072m.
Complete. Clay model of a tripod throne with a high rounded back ending up in three protrusions and down in three short, thick legs. Its back is rendered by three vertical and two horizontal strips. Grey-buff clay and slip, dark-brown paint. Simple decoration around the seat, on the back and the feet consisting of vertical and horizontal stripes and rows of dashes.
It belongs to Mylonas type B (latticed or open) without occupant (empty).
For discussion and references, see Mylonas, 'Seated and multiple Mycenaean figurines', in S. Weinberg (ed.), *The Aegean and the Near East, Studies presented to H. Goldman* (New York, 1956), 117, pl. XIV 15a; French, *BSA* 66 (1971), 167; and Divari-Valakou, in K. Demakopoulou (ed.), *Troy-Mycenae-Tiryns-Orchomenos*, (Athens 1990), 373: 362 (Tiryns).
LH IIIA.

25-387. Globular stirrup jar. Fig. 8b, Pl. 6c-d

H. 0.114m; D. 0.108m.
Complete. Reddish-brown clay and slip, black semi-lustrous paint partly worn off. Concave spout with splaying rim; flat top-disc with central elevation. Low ring base.
Concentric circles on top disc, ring around rim, encircling loop around base of spout and false neck; diagonal cross with reserved triangle on outside of handles; four groups of bands on body and around the base; shoulder decorated with papyri and accessorial solid lozenges.
FS 175, FM 11: 15; 73: (?).
Cf. Papadopoulos, *Mycenaean Achaea*, fig. 209a; Benzi, *RCM*, pls. 12: g, 27: d, 166: g.
LH IIIC Middle.

26-388. Globular stirrup jar. Not found

Pres. H. 0.096m; D. 0.078m.
Fragmentary but restored. Half of the vase missing. Pinkish clay, yellowish slip, dark-brown paint partly worn off. Ring around the base of false neck, groups of bands and fine lines on central body, the lower body and shoulder are undecorated.
FS (?).
LH IIIB (?).

27-409 Globular glass bead. Fig. 36, Pl. 26d

Cf. Iakovisis, *Perati B,* 305, fig. 128, Papadopoulos, *op. cit.*, fig. 325: 1-2.
LH III.

28-410 Conical button of steatite. Fig. 36, Pl. 26i

H. 0.016m; D. 0.021m.
Complete. Made of black steatite
See reference for No. 21-551.
LH III.

29-493. Lekythos. Fig. 9a, Pl. 7b

H. 0.078m; D. 0.074m.
Complete, but cracked. Buff-brown clay yellowish slip, black paint almost entirely worn off. Surface too ruined to determine type of decoration, but scant traces of bands on the body are visible.
FS 122.
Cf. examples listed by Furumark, *MP III*, pl. 68; Mountjoy, *MDP*, fig. 242.
LH IIIC Late.

30-494. Amphoriskos. Not found

H. 0.093m; D. 0.098m.
Broken, restored and mended. Pinkish-buff clay and slip, brown paint. Globular body, low ring base. Groups of bands and fine lines on body,
joining semicircles or scale pattern on shoulder.
FS 59, FM 42: (?) or 70: (?).
LH IIIC.

31-495. Globular jug. Fig. 10b, Pl. 7c

Pres. H. 0.061m; D. 0.073m.
Broken, partly restored, lower half of body and base lost. Pinkish-red clay, yellow slip, light to dark-brown paint, slightly worn off. Back of handle painted solid, bands on the rim, the base of neck and the body; radiated vertical bands on the shoulder.
FS 115; FM 72: 11.
Cf. examples listed by Furumark, *MP III*, pl. 64; Mountjoy, *MDP*, fig. 210; *RMDP*, fig. 218: 421 (Perati).
LH IIIC Middle.

32-496. Two joining sherds of a large vase. Pl. 7d

Pres. H. 0.22m; D. 0.18m.
Part of body and the low conical base of a big vase (three-handled piriform jar (?)). Reddish-buff clay, yellowish slip, dark-brown paint, slightly worn off. Two groups of three and two bands on body, base painted solid.
FS 34 or 35 (?).
Cf. examples listed by Furumark, *MP III*, pl. 24; Papadopoulos, *Aigion*, pls. 48, 60; Mountjoy, *op. cit.*, figs. 78, 79
LH IIIA2 (?).

TOMB C (3)

33-382. Lekythos. Fig. 10a, Pl. 7e

H. 0.112m; D. 0.11m.
Broken, restored; small parts of rim and lower body lost, but mended.
Buff-brown clay, yellowish slip, dark- to pale-brown paint. Ring around rim and base of neck, edging lines running down the back of handle, two groups of bands on body, ring base painted solid. Connected, isolated semicircles and groups of vertical wavy lines on shoulder.
FS 123; FM 42: 32; 53; 37 (?)
Cf. Papadopoulos, *Mycenaean Achaea*, figs. 147e-f, 150d.
LH IIIC Late.

34-383. Baseless askos. Fig. 11a, Pl. 8a

H. 0.075m; D. 0.101m.
Broken, restored, small part of base lost, but mended. Reddish clay, yellowish slip, red paint mostly worn off. Handle and body painted solid, apart from a narrow reserved zone at the shoulder.
FS 194.
Cf. examples listed by Furumark, *MP*, 617; Mountjoy, *RMDP*, figs. 28: 193 (Argolid), 66: 59 (Korinthia), 237: 587 (Attica), 298: 109 (Phocis), 334: 37 (Thessaly), 433: 220 (Rhodes).
LH IIIA2.

35-384. Rounded alabastron. Fig. 11b, Pl. 8b

Pres. H. 0.10m; D. 0.12m.
Partly repaired from many fragments; more than half of the body, neck and rim missing. Pinkish clay, yellowish slip, red paint mostly worn off. Monochrome (?). FS 85 (?).
Cf. examples listed by Furumark, MP III, pl. 50; Mountjoy, MDP, fig. 83; Papadopoulos, Mycenaean Achaea, figs. 132g, 133h; Giannopoulos 2008, pl. 33: 60, π10426.
LH IIIA1-2.

36-385. Squat stirrup jar. Fig. 9c, Pl.8c

H. 0.113m; D. 0.139m.
Complete. Pinkish clay, yellow slip, light-brown paint. Perked-up squat globular shape. Almost straight spout with flaring rim about equal in height to false neck; convex top disc; relatively broad base with a low ring foot. Concentric circles with large central dot on top disc; ring around rim, encircling loop around base of spout and false neck; two groups of bands enclosing fine lines on lower shoulder and body; handles and base painted solid; upper shoulder decorated with semicircular multiple stem.
FS 180; FM 19: 29.
Cf. examples listed by Furumark, MP, 614; Papadopoulos, Aigion, pls. 30, 50, 91; Mycenaean Achaea, fig. 116a-b; Mountjoy, MDP, fig. 130: 1; RMDP, figs. 34: 252, 253 (Argolid), 70: 130 (Korinthia), 93: 149 (Laconia), 257: 131, 132 (Boeotia), 298: 102, 103 (Phocis), 415: 91, 92 (Rhodes).
LH IIIB1.

37-389. Globular stirrup jar. Fig. 12b, Pl. 8d-e

H. 0.112m; D. 0.113m.
Broken at base of spout, but restored, body slightly chipped, otherwise complete. Pinkish clay, yellowish slip, dark-brown paint partly worn off. Globular body, low ring base, spout leaning slightly outwards with splayed lip. Concentric circles on convex top disc, ring at top of spout, encircling loop at base of spout and false neck; lower body and outside of base painted solid; diagonal cross outside of handles; shoulder decorated with concentric semicircles, vertical parallel chevrons and a panelled pattern (triglyph) of zig-zag.
FS 175; FM 43: 4; 58: 22; 61: 18.
Cf. examples listed by Furumark, MP III, pl. 99; Papadopoulos, Mycenaean Achaea, fig. 98d, f; Mountjoy, MDP, fig. 181; RMDP, figs. 151: 101 (Achaea).
LH IIIC Early.

38- 390. Globular stirrup jar. Pl. 9a

H. 0.12m; D. 0.116m.
Complete and intact. Pinkish clay, red-brown slip, brown paint. Globular body, low ring base, vertical spout with splayed lip. Circle and spiral on flat top disc, rings around the lip of spout and base of false neck, outside of handles barred. A group of successive bands on upper body, the lower body and base painted solid; fringed isolated concentric semicircles on shoulder zone.
FS 175; FM 43: (p?).
Cf. examples listed by Furumark, *op. cit.*; Papadopoulos, *op. cit.*, fig. 77e-f; Mountjoy, *RMDP*, fig. 450: 85 (Kos).
LH IIIC Late.

39-391. Globular stirrup jar. Fig. 8a, Pl. 9c-d

H. 0.155m; D. 0.151m.
The spout is lost, the surface is considerably rubbed. What remains is unbroken. Pinkish clay, reddish-brown slip, dark-brown to black paint slightly worn off. Globular body, ring base. Spiral with central dot on the coned top disc, encircling loop around the base of spout and false neck, outside of handles have edging lines with their central part left blank. Group of successive bands on upper body and another enclosing fine lines on lower body, base painted solid. On shoulder zone three hatched triangles, another with horizontal wavy lines, vertical chevrons and joining semicircles.
FS 176; FM 61A: 6; 58: 22; 42: 4
Cf. examples listed by Furumark, *op. cit.*, pl. 100; Mountjoy, *RMDP*, fig. 311: 281 (Phocis).
LH IIIC Middle.

40-392. Globular jug. Fig. 9b, Pl. 9b

H. 0.141m; D. 0.123m.
Broken, restored, otherwise complete. Reddish clay, dark-brown to red slip and paint partly worn off. Globular body, ribbon-type handle, low ring handle. Monochrome.
FS 112.
Cf. Papadopoulos, *Mycenaean Achaea*, figs. 152a, 246a; Mountjoy, *MDP*, fig. 85; *RMDP*, fig. 164: 45-48; Kontorli-Papadopoulou, *AM* 118 (2003), figs. 17-18.
LH IIIA2 Early.

41-393. Straight-sided alabastron. Pl. 10a

H. 0.096m; D. 0.097m.
Neck broken but restored, otherwise complete. Pinkish clay, buff slip, reddish paint slightly worn off. Narrow concave neck, with flat horizontal rim; angular shoulder and cylindrical body, slightly convex base; two loop handles set opposite each other horizontally on shoulder; neck painted solid, running spiral on shoulder, broad bands enclosing fine lines on body; handles barred.
FS 96; FM 46: 58.
Cf. Papadopoulos, *op. cit.*, figs. 143e, 144f; Giannopoulos 2008, pls. 20: 12, 22: 16, 24: 28-30, 25: 34; Mountjoy, *MDP*, fig. 173: 1; *RMDP*, figs. 121: 123-124 (Messenia), 138: 83 (Elis), 209: 328, 330 (Attica); 282: 22-28 (Skyros); 425: 165-167 (Rhodes); 450: 76 (Kos).
LH IIIC Early.

42-394. Straight-sided alabastron. Pl. 10b

H. 0.085m; D. 0.10m.
Complete and intact but the surface is slightly worn. Pinkish clay, red-brown slip, red paint, partly worn off. Shape similar to No. 41-393. The exterior surface is banded and there are two bands inside the neck. Handles painted solid.
FS 96.
See references for No. 41-393.
LH IIIC Early.

43-395. Six conical steatite buttons. Fig. 36, Pl. 26j

Ranging in H. from 0.011m to 0.015m and in D. from 0.014m to 0.026m. They are complete and made of black (a, c), purple (b, f) and grey-buff steatite, polished and undecorated.
See references for No.21-551.
LH III.

44-411. Two steatite buttons. Fig. 36, Pl. 26k

H. 0.013m and 0.015m; D. 0.017m and 0.017m.
Complete. Made of polished black steatite; in shape one is conical the other shanked.
For references of the conical artefact, see No.21-551, and for the shanked find, see Furumark, *CMP*, 89, fig. 2: b.
LH III.

45-412. Bronze ring. Fig. 36, Pl. 26l

D. of hoop 0.021m.
Complete. Plain circular shape.
Cf. Papadopoulos, *Aigion*, figs. 54, 63; *Mycenaean Achaea*, fig. 324a.
LH.

46-413. Bronze 'violin-bow' fibula. Fig. 36, Pl. 26m

L. 0.083m; W. 0.013m; H. 0.025m.
Broken, but restored and complete. The metal is severely oxidized. Bow and pin are parallel with a catch-plate, but the greater part of the bow is hammered into a flat, approximately elliptical (leaf-shaped), platform, whose upper surface is decorated with four plastic dots set in a cross-rhomboid arrangement. It belongs to Blinkenberg 'Types myceniens', Furumark 'Simple fiddle-bow type', Kilian type I, and Sapouna-Sakellarakis type Ie.
Blinkenberg, *Fibules*, 49-54; Furumark, *CMP*, 91, fig. 3: 7-8; Kilian, *Fibeln I*, 18, pl. 1: 1, 5 (Thessaly); Sapouna-Sakellarakis, *Fibeln II*, 37-38, pls. 1: 21-23, 2: 24-28.
LH IIIB.

47-475. Globular jug. Fig. 13a, Pl. 10c

H. 0.076m; D. 0.076m.
Complete. Pinkish clay, red-brown slip, dark-brown paint slightly worn off. Globular body, cylindrical handle, low ring base. Monochrome.
FS 111.
Cf. examples listed by Furumark, *MP III*, pl. 63; Papadopoulos, *Mycenaean Achaea*, fig. 154d-e; Mountjoy, *RMDP*, fig. 164: 45-48; Wardle 1972, fig. 99: 44; Brodbeck-Jucker 1986, fig. 8: 20-23 (Kephallenia).
LH IIIC Late.

48-476. Amphoriskos. Fig. 13c, Pl. 10d

H. 0.085m; D. 0.094m.
Broken chips from the rim, one handle lost; pinkish clay smoothed inside and out, yellow slip, red-brown paint. Globular body, lipless rim, two strap horizontal handles, raised concave base. Solid paint inside the neck, broad band at its base; in the handle zone two horizontal wavy lines, horizontal stripes on handles, lower body painted solid, base reserved.
FS 59; FM 53: 21.
Cf. examples listed by Furumark, *op. cit.*, pl. 38; Papadopoulos, *op. cit.*, fig. 159d-h; Giannopoulos 2008, pls. 22: 14-15; 75: 6 (Achaea); Brodbeck-Jucker, *op. cit.*, fig. 1: 4-7 (Kephallenia); Mountjoy, *MDP*, fig. 167: 1; *RMDP*, figs. 40: 303-306 (Argolid),

135: 65-66I (Elis), 163: 21-32 (Kephallenia), 208: 309-314 (Attica), 282: 8-17 (Skyros), 423: 136-151 (Rhodes), 449: 71(Kos).
LH IIIC Early.

49-477. Globular stirrup jar. Pl. 11a

H. 0.174m; D. 0.172m.
Repaired from many fragments; broken chips from the rim of spout, small parts of the body lost, but restored. Light brick-red clay, pale-yellow slip, dark-brown paint, partly worn off. Globular-biconical body, spout lower than the top disc of false neck, leaning slightly outwards with splaying lip. Ring base, strap handles. Flat top disc with a central conical nipple and handles painted solid; lip of spout painted inside and out, encircling loop around the base of spout and false neck; handle zone decorated with connected concentric semicircles and spirals; Rest of the body and base painted solid.
FS 176; FM 43: 34; 46: 56.
Cf. examples listed by Furumark, *op. cit.*, pl. 100; Papadopoulos, *op. cit.*, fig. 215d; Brodbeck-Jucker, *op. cit.*, fig. 9:29; Mountjoy, *RMDP*, fig. 165: 59 (Kephallenia).
LH IIIC Late.

50-478. Globular-baggy jug. Fig. 13b, Pl. 11b

H. 0.069m; D. 0.083m.
Repaired from many fragments; neck and large part of body lost and restored. Pinkish clay, pale-yellow slip, dark-brown paint much rubbed. Globular-baggy body, round handle, ring base slightly concave underside. Handle painted solid; two horizontal series of dots on handle zone, two groups of bands on body, outside of base painted solid.
FS 114; FM 41: 7 (?).
Cf. examples listed by Furumark, *op. cit.*, pl. 64; Papadopoulos, *Mycenaean Achaea*, fig. 153e; Mountjoy, *MDP*, fig. 121; *RMDP*, fig. 188: 136-138 (Attica).
LH IIIA2/B1.

51-479. Globular stirrup jar. Fig. 30b, Pl. 11c-d

H. 0.118m; D. 0.117m.
Upper part of spout is lost, small part of body missing but restored and the surface is a good deal rubbed. What remains is unbroken. Red-brick clay, light-brown slip, reddish paint mostly worn off. Depressed globular body, convex top disc with central conical nipple, thickened strap handles, torus foot. Concentric circles on top disc, encircling loop around the base of spout and false neck; traces of paint on handles; one band and two fine lines below shoulder zone,

which is decorated with isolated concentric semicircles and double straight lines between them in the semicircle; lower body and outside of base painted solid.
FS 175; FM 43: d.
Cf. examples listed by Furumark, *op. cit.*, pl. 99; Papadopoulos, *op. cit.*, figs. 87d, 215:a; Mountjoy, *RMDP*, figs. 60: 463 (Argolid); 311: 279 (Phocis).
LH IIIC Middle.

52-480. Globular stirrup jar. Fig. 14a, Pl. 12a

H. 0.13m; D. 0.129m.
Repaired from many fragments; parts of top disc and body lost but restored. Pinkish clay, brown slip, reddish paint mostly worn off. Globular body, convex-flattish top disc, thickened strap handles, ring handles. The spout has paint on the lip, solid circle on the centre of top disc, ring around its perimeter, encircling loop band around the base of spout and false neck; The handles are painted solid. Handle zone framed below by a band decorated with hatched triangles, blank zone below, belly zone painted with horizontal quirk pattern, bands on lower body and outside the base.
FS 175; FM 61A: 6: 48: 5.
Cf. examples listed by Furumark, *op. cit.*; Papadopoulos, *op. cit.*, fig. 208d-e; Mountjoy, *RMDP*, figs. 46: 347 (Argolid), 166: 61 (Kephallenia), 311: 281, 312: 287 (Phocis).
LH IIIC Early.

53-481. Four conical steatite buttons. Fig. 36

H. 0.013-0.018m; W. 0.015-0.023m.
Complete. Two are made of pale green and the other two of purple steatite. Undecorated.
See references for No. 21-551.
LH III.

TOMB D (4)

54-398. Amphoriskos. Fig. 15a , Pl. 12b

H. 0.106m; D. 0.117m.
Complete. Pinkish clay, red-brown paint, partly worn off. Globular shape with sloping shoulders, short flaring neck and a lipless rim; two round horizontal handles just above the belly; raised concave base. Monochrome.
FS 59.
Cf. examples listed by Furumark, *op. cit.,* pl. 38; Papadopoulos, *op. cit.*, figs. 156: 326, 157: 248 (Achaea); Brodbeck-Jucker 1986, fig. 4: 9 (Kephallenia); 208: 314 (Attica); 282: 17 (Skyros).
LH IIIC Early.

55-399. Globular stirrup jar. Fig. 14b, Pl. 12c

H. 0.117m; D. 0.112m.
Most of rim of spout is lost. What remains is complete and intact. Globular shape, torus foot, the underside concave on lip of spout, inside and out; spiral on top disc, encircling loop around; spout somewhat lower than the disc of the flat false neck; handles of strap section. Pinkish-buff clay, glossy dark-brown paint partly worn off. Paint the base of spout and false neck; handles painted solid. In the shoulder zone, concentric semicircles and fringed line-triglyph between them; the shoulder zone is marked off by a group of medium encircling bands; a broad band on the lower body and outside of base.
FS 176; FM 43: J; 75: (?).
Cf. examples listed by Furumark, *op. cit.*, pl. 100.
LH IIIC Middle.

56-400. Conical stirrup jar. Fig. 15b, Pl. 12d-e

H. 0.099m; D. 0.124m.
Part of the top disc and one handle lost, but restored. Body is slightly chipped; otherwise complete. Conical shape with rounded shoulder with almost flat top; the spout is tall and narrow with a rounded rim; torus base. Scant traces of concentric circles or spirals on the disc of false neck; rings at the base of the false neck and spout and at the lip of the spout. Sea-anemones on shoulder zone; banding down the body, consisting of fine line groups flanked by single broad bands; broad band around the base and concentric circles on the underside.
FS 182; FM 27: 14.
Cf. Papadopoulos, *Mycenaean Achaea,* figs. 117f-I, 118a-d; Mountjoy, *MDP*, fig. 131; *RMDP*, figs. 34: 255 (Argolid), 70: 131 (Korinthia); 134: 60 (Elis); 199: 229-231 (Attica); 257: 134 (Boeotia); 298: 104-107 (Phocis); 415: 93-94 (Rhodes); 446: 50 (Kos).
LH IIIB1.

57-401. Rounded alabastron. Fig. 16b, Pl. 13a

H. 0.055m; D. 0.09m.
Handles and part of the neck lost; significant cracking on the body, the surface is a good deal rubbed. Brick-red clay and slip, reddish paint, almost totally worn off. Baggy shape with a short concave neck terminating in a short sloping lip; three horizontal round handles (?); base slightly concave underneath. Neck monochrome outside, rock pattern on the shoulder, concentric circles around and underneath the base.
FS 85; FS 32: 5.
Cf. Papadopoulos, *op. cit.*, fig. 129d-h; Mountjoy, *MDP*, fig. 83; *RMDP*, figs. 24: 150, 153 (Argolid), 113: 64 (Messenia), 187: 130 (Attica), 252: 76 (Boeotia), 291: 40 (Phocis), 320: 27-28 (Aitolo-Akarnania), 338: 66-70 (Thessaly), 403: 24-25 (Rhodes), 443: 19 (Kos).
LH IIIA2.

58-402. Straight-sided alabastron. Fig. 16a, Pls. 13c-d

H. 0.102m; D. 0.132m.
Rim chipped, concave neck cracked, large surface scar on body, otherwise complete. Pinkish clay, yellowish slip, red paint partly worn off. Cylindrical shape with a sloping shoulder; two loop handles set opposite each other horizontally on shoulder; lower body slightly tapering towards the base. Neck painted solid inside and out; a chain of lozenges in the handle zone framed by bands above and below; Strap horizontal handles banded. Panelled pattern framed by two bands on lower body consisting of antithetic spiral, zig-zag and concentric semicircles on one side and antithetic spiral and fringed chequers on the other.
FS 98; FM 73: 3; 50: 16 (?); 19 (?).
Cf. examples listed by Furumark, *op. cit.*, pl. 54; Papadopoulos, *op. cit.*, fig. 145f-g; *RMDP*, figs. 123: 132 (Messenia), 138: 86 (Elis).
LH IIIC Late.

59-403. Clay button. Fig. 36, Pls. 16n

H. 0.025m; D. base 0.027m.
Complete. Grey-buff clay; conical shape.
See references for No. 3-411.
LH II.

60-418. Kylix. Fig. 17a, Pl. 13b

H. 0.085m; D. 0.083m.
Repaired from fragments; parts of wall lost. Brick-red clay, dark-brown to red paint mostly worn off. Deep semi-globular bowl, carving slightly inwards at the lip; a high-swung ring handle; short thick stem, heavy, conical and articulated into a dome underneath base. Monochrome.
FS 271 (?).
Cf. examples listed by Furumark, *op. cit.*, pl. 148.
LH IIB.

61-419. Amphoriskos. Fig. 18a, Pl. 14a

H. 0.073m; D. 0.075m.
Broken, repaired from fragments; one handle lost. Pinkish clay and slip, brown-buff paint partly worn off. Globular shape with sloping shoulders, short flaring neck and lipless rim; disc-shaped base. Paint on neck and lip inside and out; handle painted solid; scant traces of decoration on shoulder; broad bands at base of handle-zone and lower body. Base painted solid.
FS 59; FM (?).
Cf. examples listed by Furumark, *op. cit.*, pl. 38; Papadopoulos, *Mycenaean Achaea*, fig. 157a, h; Mountjoy, *RMDP*, figs. 42: 325-327 (Argolid); 208: 311, 314 (Attica).
LH IIIC Early.

62-420. Amphoriskos. Fig. 18b, Pl. 14b

H. 0.076m; D. 0.089m.
Complete and intact, but the surface is a good deal scarred. Pinkish clay, yellowish slip, red paint partly worn off. Dumpy-baggy body, wide mouth, round handles set high on the shoulder, wide base. Mouth painted inside and out; simple, horizontal zig-zag on handle zone, wide bands on the body; concentric circles underneath the base.
FS 59; FM 61: 2.
Cf. Papadopoulos, *op. cit.*, fig. 251b; Mountjoy, *op. cit.*, figs. 40: 304 (Argolid), 163: 25 (Kephallenia).
LH IIIC Early.

63-421. Amphoriskos. Fig. 18c, Pl. 14c

H. 0.107m; D. 0.112m.
One handle lost, otherwise complete and intact. Pinkish clay, pale slip, yellowish paint. Globular-ovoid shape, wide concave neck, sloping rim, round horizontal handles just above the belly; raised concave base. Rim painted solid, handles barred, Handle zone decorated with single zig-zag framed by bands above and below; base painted solid.
FS 59; FM 61: 2.
See references for No. 62-420.
LH IIIC Early.

64-422. Straight-sided alabastron Fig. 17b, Pl. 14d

H. 0.093m; D. 0.103m.
Rim and body slightly chipped; otherwise complete and intact. Pinkish clay, pale-yellow slip, dark-brown paint. Straight-sided cylindrical body, concave neck, lipless rim; two round horizontal handles, convex base. Neck and handles monochrome, body banded, concentric circles underneath the base.
FS 96.
Cf. examples listed by Furumark, *op. cit.*, pl. 54; Papadopoulos, *op. cit.*, fig. 145b, f.; Mountjoy, *op. cit.*, figs. 138: 83 (Elis), 209: 331-332 (Attica), 282: 26-28 (Skyros), 455: 125 (Kos).
LII IIIC Early.

65-423. Steatite button. Pls. 16o

H. 0.015m; D. 0.028m.
Complete. Conical shape, dark purple steatite. Undecorated.
See references for No. 21-551.
LH III.

66-424. Globular jug. Pl. ? not found

H. 0.069m; D. 0.067m.
Complete and intact, but the surface is slightly worn. Pinkish clay, dark-brown paint. Globular shape, concave neck, round vertical handle rising slightly above rim, ring base. Monochrome.
FS 113.
Cf. examples listed by Furumark, *MP III*, pl. 63; Mountjoy, *MDP*, fig. 85: 2; *RMDP*, fig. 24: 165 (Argolid).
LH IIIA2.

67-425. Globular jug. Fig. 19a, Pl. 15a

H. 0.079m; D. 0.08.
Complete and intact. Fine buff-yellow clay and slip, brown paint much worn off. Globular shape, concave neck, round vertical handle rising slightly above rim; ring base. Neck, base and handle painted solid; body banded.
FS 113.
Cf. examples listed for No. 66-424.
LH III A2.

68-426. Amphoriskos. Fig. 19b, Pl. 15b

H. 0.086m; D. 0.099m.
Repaired from many fragments; rim chipped. Pinkish clay, buff-brown slip, red paint, mostly worn off. Globular-baggy shape, short, flaring neck, lipless rim; two round horizontal handles just above the belly; raised concave base; neck monochrome inside and plain outside, Handle zone decorated with simple zig-zag framed by wide bands above and below; base painted solid.
FS 59; FM. 61: 2.
See references for No. 62-420.
LH IIIC Early.

69-427. Straight-sided alabastron. Fig. 20a, Pl. 15c

H. 0.067m; D. 0.08m.
Rim and body chipped, otherwise complete. Brick-red clay, pale-yellow slip, red paint, slightly worn off. Cylindrical lower body with sloping shoulders; short, concave neck with a rounded lipless rim; two strap loop handles applied to the lower body; flat concave base. The neck is monochrome inside and out, multiple splashes on the handles. Foliate band on the handle zone framed above and below by two bands; body banded.
FS 96; FM 64: 21.
Cf. examples listed by Furumark, *MP III*, pl. 54; Mountjoy, *RMDP*, figs. 138: 83 (Elis), 147: 70 (Achaea), 209: 332 (Attica), 282: 26, 28 (Skyros), 344: 115-116 (Thessaly), 425: 165-167 (Rhodes).
LH IIIC Early.

70-428. Based, straight-sided alabastron. Fig. 20b, Pl. 15d

H. 0.087m; D. 0.097m.
Complete. Pale buff clay and slip, dark brown paint mostly worn off. Cylindrical lower body with sloping shoulders; short concave neck with a lipless rim; two round handles attached to the lower shoulder, low ring base. Rim painted, broad

band on the neck outside, inside left plain; splash on the handles. Handle zone decorated with horizontal parallel chevrons, body and ring base banded.
FS 97; FM. 58: 36.
Cf. examples listed by Furumark, *MP III*, pl. 55; Mountjoy, *RMDP*, figs. 43: 331 (Argolid), 99: 232 (Laconia), 209: 333 (Attica), 261: 175 (Boeotia), 282: 29 (Skyros), 425: 168-170 (Rhodes), 450: 77 (Kos).
LH IIIC Early.

71-429. Based askos. Fig. 20cc, Pl. 16a

H. 0.099m; D. 0.83m.
Upper part of spout lost, base chipped, otherwise complete. Pinkish clay, dull creamy-yellow slip, dark-brown paint partly worn off. Globular-ovoid shape, slightly oblique spout and a flattened loop handle with both joints on top of the body in line with spout; ring concave base. Rings around the spout, encircling loop around the base of spout and handle, single horizontal wavy line on shoulder; lower body, base and handle banded.
FS 195; FM 53: 19.
Cf. examples listed by Furumark, *op. cit.*, pl. 113; Papadopoulos, *Mycenaean Achaea*, fig. 162d; Mountjoy, *op. cit.*, figs. 70: 139 (Argolid), 114: 74 (Messenia), 190: 155 (Attica), 334: 38 (Thessaly), 357: 34 (Kea), 365: 29 (Melos) 411: 43 (Rhodes). Also, Benzi, *RCM*, 108 and notes 43-47.
LH IIIB/C Early.

72-430. Globular stirrup jar. Fig. 21b, Pl. 16b

H. 0.097m; D. 0.086m.
One handle lost, spout broken at its base but restored; rim of spout and top disc chipped, the surface is a good deal rubbed. Pinkish-buff clay, yellowish slip, dark-brown paint mostly worn off. Globular shape, narrow false neck with a flat disc; slightly oblique, narrow spout with lipless rim, raised concave base. Circle and central dot on top disc; two separate rings at base of spout and false neck; handles painted solid, two series of dots on shoulder; broad bands and fine lines on body and outside the base.
FS 176; FM. 41: 4 (?).
Cf. examples listed by Furumark, *op. cit.*, pl. 100; Papadopoulos, *op. cit.*, fig. 208b.
LH IIIB1.

73-431. Globular stirrup jar. Fig. 21A, Pl. 16c-d

H. 0.123m; D. 0.112m.
Repaired from fragments; spout, belly and base slightly chipped, otherwise complete. Brick-red clay and slip, dark-brown to black paint, partly worn off. Globular shape, spout leaning slightly outwards with splaying lip, low ring base. Concave top disc and strap handles painted solid; separate rings on rim of spout, at its base and the base of false neck. Shoulder blank, three wide uneven bands on body.
FS 171.
Cf. Papadopoulos, *op. cit.*, 75 (six examples); Mountjoy, *RMDP*, figs. 47: 357 (Argolid), 96: 190 (Korinthia), 132: 43 (Laconia), 261: 180 (Boeotia), 283: 41,42 (Skyros), 311: 283 (Phocis), 446: 49 (Kos).
LH IIIA2.

74-432. Squat-globular stirrup jar. Fig. 22A, Pl. 17a-b

H. 0.11m; D. 0.115m.
Body and lip of spout slightly chipped; otherwise complete and intact. Pinkish clay, red-brown slip, dark- to pale-brown paint. Perked-up squat globular body, vertical spout with strongly horizontal lip; raised base. Base and outside of handles painted solid except for a reserved triangle next to top disc; encircling loop at base of spout and false neck, lip painted inside and out; concentric circles with central dot on top disc. On body groups of bands and fine lines to line of spout attachment. Quirk pattern on shoulder zone.
FS 180; FM 48: 8.
Cf. examples listed by Furumark, *MP III*, pl. 104; Papadopoulos, *op. cit.*, fig. 116a; *Aigion*, pls. 37b, 59b, 96b; Kontorli-Papadopoulou 2003, 31, fig. 8(Aigeira), Mountjoy, *RMDP*, figs. 34: 252, 253 (Argolid), 70: 130 (Korinthia), 93: 149 (Laconia), 198: 228 (Attica), 257: 131, 132 (Boeotia), 298: 103 (Phocis), 369: 104 (Melos), 415: 91, 92 (Rhodes), 446: 49 (Kos).
LH IIIB1.

75-433. Amphoriskos. Fig. 22b, Pl. 17c

H. 0.085m; D. 0.096m.
Repaired from many fragments; one handle lost, parts of neck and rim missing but restored. Pinkish clay, pale-yellow slip, red paint mostly worn off. Globular shape, short, flaring neck, lipless rim; two horizontal handles just above the belly; raised concave base. Base and outside of handles painted solid; multiple stem hooked on shoulder framed by two bands above and three below, the uppermost fringed.
FS 59; FM 19: 58.
Cf. examples listed by Furumark, *MP III*, pl. 38.
LH IIIC Early.

76-434. Amphoriskos. Fig. 23a, Pl. 17d

H. 0.097m; D. 0.093m.
Repaired from many fragments, small part lost but restored. Buff-brown clay, pale-yellow slip, light-brown paint. Globular body, short, flaring neck with lipless rim; two horizontal handles just above the belly; base raised concave. Dotted rim, wide bands inside and outside the neck; zig-zag pattern on the narrow handle zone continued on the back of handles, framed by bands above and below; base painted solid.
FS 59; FM 61; 2.
See references for No. 62-420.
LH IIIC Early.

77-435. Amphoriskos. Fig. 23b, Pl 18a

H. 0.108m; D. 0.102m.
Repaired from many fragments; parts of the body and one handle lost. Pinkish-buff clay, yellowish slip, dark-brown to black paint partly worn off. Globular-ovoid body, concave neck with lipless rim; two horizontal handles placed on the belly; narrow ring base. Neck, handles and base painted solid; groups of bands and fine lines on the body, on the narrow handle zone single wavy line on one side and quirk on the opposite.
FS 59; FM 53: 19; 48: 5.
See references for No. 62-420; Mountjoy, *RMDP*, figs. 423: 139-140 (Rhodes).
LH IIIC Middle.

78-436. Squat-globular stirrup jar. Fig. 24a, Pl. 18b

H. 0.071m; D. 0.073m.
Repaired from many fragments; one handle and two parts of body are lost and the surface is a good deal chipped and rubbed. Pinkish clay and slip, dark-brown to black paint partly worn off. Squat globular-ovoid
shape, concave top disc, lipless spout slightly leaning outwards, strap handles, ring base concave underneath. Spiral on top disc, rim of spout painted inside and out, two separate fringed rings around the base of spout and the false neck; barred handle. Concentric semicircles, fringed circles with dots inside on shoulder, one wide band and fine lines on body and around the base.
FS 171; FM 43: 4; 41: (?).
Cf. examples listed by Furumark, *MP III*, pl. 97; Papadopoulos, *Mycenaean Achaea*, figs. 208e, 210e, f, 211a, 217d.
LH IIIC Early.

79-437. Globular stirrup jar. Fig. 24b, Pl. 18c-d

H. 0.106m; D. 0.087m.
Restored from many pieces with large parts of body missing. Pale-buff clay and slip, red-brown paint partly worn off. Perked-up globular shape, flat top disc, lipless spout leaning outwards, strap handles, ring base concave underneath. Spiral on top disc, rim of spout painted inside and out, encircling loop around the base of spout and false neck; barred handles. Groups of dots separated by a vertical wavy line starting from the encircling loop and net pattern on shoulder; four wide bands on body and around the base, the underneath of which is decorated with a simple cross.
FS 173; FM 41: (?); 53: (?); 57: 2; 54: (?).
Cf. examples listed by Furumark, *MP III*, pl. 98; Papadopoulos, *op. cit.*, figs. 210d.
LH IIIB1.

80-438. Globular stirrup jar. Fig. 25a, Pl. 19a

H. 0.105m; D. 0.10m.
Repaired from fragments, with a small part of the body lost and spout and base chipped. Reddish clay, reddish-yellow slip, brown to reddish-brown paint mostly worn off. Perked-up globular shape, flat top disc, lipless spout, narrow strap handles, ring base concave underneath. Single circle on top disc, rim of spout painted inside and out, encircling loop around the base of spout and false neck. The handles are 'laddered' by irregular horizontal strokes. Groups of dots on shoulder, broad encircling band beneath; on the belly a single wavy line framed by two fine lines above and below, three bands on the lower body, base painted solid, simple cross on its underside.
FS 173; FM 41: (?); 53: 17; 54: (?).
Cf. examples listed by Furumark, *op. cit.*; for decoration with groups of dots, see preceding No. 79-437.
LH IIIB1.

81-439. Globular stirrup jar. Fig. 25b, Pl. 19b

H. 0.115m; D. 0.106m
Restored from many pieces with a small part of body missing. Buff clay, yellowish slip, brown paint, partly worn off. Perked-up globular body, flat top disc, spout leaning slightly outwards, strap handles, low ring base concave underneath. Concentric circles with central dot on top disc; ring on inner surface of lip of spout; encircling loop at base of spout and false neck. Handles decorated with edging lines; triangular patches of joining semicircles on shoulder, circles with

central dot on belly zone below handles; scant traces of isolated zig-zag below the belly zone; lower body banded, base painted solid.
FS 173; FM 42: 21; 41: (?); 61A: 1.
Cf. examples listed for preceding vase (No. **80-438**); Papadopoulos, *op. cit.*, figs. 104h. 211j, 206a; Mountjoy, *RMDP*, figs. 53: 399 (Argolid), 415: 93 (Rhodes).
LH III B1.

82-440. Piriform stirrup jar. Fig. 26A, Pl. 19c

H. 0.137m; D. 0.12m.
Restored from many pieces with a large part of body lost. Reddish clay, yellowish slip, dark-brown to black paint, mostly worn off. Tall conical-piriform shape, flat top disc, spout leaning slightly outwards with a rounded lip, strap handles, torus disc base, concave underneath. Concentric circles with central dot on top disc; lip of spout painted inside and out; separate rings around the base of spout and false neck. Edging lines with reserved triangle on top of handles; triangular patches of dots on shoulder, horizontal chain of zig-zag on belly zone; two broad bands on lower body and around the base.
FS 167; FM 41: (?); 61: 4.
Cf. examples listed by Furumark, *MP III*, pl. 94; for decoration on the shoulder with dots see above Nos. 79-437 and 80-438.
LH IIIB1.

83-441. Piriform stirrup jar. Fig. 26b, Pl. 19d

H. 0.131m; D. 0.11m.
Restored from many pieces with large parts of body missing. Pinkish-buff clay, yellow slip, dark-brown to black paint mostly worn off. Conical-piriform body, flat top disc, tubular spout slightly leaning outwards with a rounded lip, strap handles, torus disc base concave underneath. Concentric circles with central dot on top disc; lip of spout painted inside and out; encircling loop around the base of spout and false neck; handles painted solid along their backs except for a small reserved triangle next to the top disc; triangular patches of dots on shoulder, horizontal chain of zig-zag on belly zone, two bands on lower body, base painted solid.
FS 167; FM 41: (?); 61: 4.
See references for preceding example (No. 83-441).
LH IIIB1.

84-442. Steatite button. Fig. 36

H. 0.014m; D. base 0.016m.
Complete. Conical shape, greyish-green steatite. Undecorated.
For references, see No. 21-551.
LH III.

85-443. Globular stirrup jar. Fig. 6a, Pl. 20a-b

H. 0.123m; D. 0.126m.
Restored from many fragments with one handle, half of the other lost and many parts of the body missing. Pale-buff clay and slip, dark-brown to black paint mostly worn off. Globular body, tubular spout slightly leaning outwards with a rounded lip, strap handles, ring base. Lip of spout painted inside and out, encircling loop around the base of spout and the false neck; horizontal strokes on backs of the handles; successive triangles and triangular diaper net on the shoulder quadrants, dotted Mycenaean flower on the semicircle; a group of bands below the handles, lower body banded, base painted solid.
FS 171; FM 61A: 1, 7; 18: (?).
Cf. examples listed by Furumark, *MP III*, pl. 97; Papadopoulos, *Mycenaean Achaea*, fig. 223g.
LH IIIA2.

86-444. Rounded alabastron. Fig. 27b, Pl. 21c

H. 0.069m; D. 0.084m.
Repaired from many fragments with large parts of neck and body lost. Yellow-buff clay and slip, dark-brown to black paint, mostly worn off. Concave neck with lipless rim; globular-baggy body, two loop handles, round base. Neck painted solid inside and out. Encircling band on junction of neck and body, handles painted solid; handle zone decorated with multiple stem, lower body painted with broad and fine lines, underneath the base concentric circles with central dot.
FS 85; FM 19: 28; 41: 16.
Cf examples listed by Furumark, *MP III*, pl. 50; Papadopoulos, *op. cit.*, fig. 135i.
LH IIIA2/B1.

87-488. Based askos. Fig. 28a, Pl. 20c-d

H. 0.089m; D. 0.095m.
Restored from many fragments; large parts of body missing. Pinkish-buff clay and slip, brown paint, slightly worn off. Globular-ovoid shape, slightly oblique spout and a flattened loop handle with both joints on top of the body in line with spout; ring concave base. Rim of spout painted inside, ring round its base, encircling loop around the base of handle the back of which is painted solid, double lozenges on shoulder; belly banded, lower body and base reserved.
FS 195; FM 73: h.
Cf. examples listed by Furumark, *op. cit.*, pl.113 and for references, see No. 71-429.
LH IIIB1.

88-489. Globular (?) stirrup jar. Fig. 29, Pl . 21a-b

Pres. H. 0.07m; D. 0.094m.
Only the upper part of the vase is preserved; pinkish clay, yellow-buff slip, dark-brown paint. Globular (?) shape, tubular spout slightly leaning outwards with a rounded lip, flat top disc, narrow strap handles. Concentric circles with central dot on top disc; ring around the lip of spout, encircling loop round the base of spout and false neck; handles painted solid, Mycenaean flower on shoulder, broad bands and fine lines below handle zone.
FS 173 (?); FM 18: 103.
Cf. examples listed by Furumark, *MP III*, pl. 98; Mountjoy, *RMDP*, figs. 115: 82 (Messenia), 145: 44 (Achaea), 256: 129 (Boeotia), 297: 98-100 (Phocis), 415: 90 (Rhodes).
LH IIIA2.

89-490. Stemmed bowl (?)

Pres. H. 0.042m; D. rim 0.137m.
Five joining fragments preserve part of the upper body and one of the two horizontal angular handles below the rim. Pinkish clay, undecorated.
FS 304 (?).
LH IIIA2.

90-491. Steatite buttons. Fig. 36

H. (a) 0.023m, (b) 0.017m; D. base (a) 0.027m, (b) 0.024m.
Two conical buttons made of (a) purple and (b) brown-buff polished steatite, vertically pierced.
For references, see No. 21-551.
LH III.

91-492. Fragment of large piriform jar.

Dim. 0.08 x 0.056 x 0.010m.
Pinkish clay, yellow slip, red-brown paint. Decorated with groups of curved and angular lines between rows of plastic knobs.
FS 34 (?); FM 19: 26, 15.
Cf. Papadopoulos, *Aigion*, pls. 48, 60.
LH IIIA2 Early.

UNPROVENANCED TOMB

92-552. Rounded alabastron. Fig. 28b, Pl. 21d

H. 0.072m; D. 0.134m.
Broken, restored, complete except for fragments from neck.
Pinkish-buff clay, yellowish slip, red-yellow paint, partly worn off.
Slightly convex-flat base; three horizontal loop handles. Neck and handles painted solid. Band around base of neck. Shoulder decorated with rock pattern and sea-anemone; encircling bands and lines at lower bower body; concentric circles on base.
FS 84; FM 32: 5; 27: 15.
Cf. examples listed by Furumark, *MP III*, pl. 49; Papadopoulos, *Mycenaean Achaea*, figs. 130c, 131g, 132b-c; Mountjoy, *RMDP*, figs. 87: 79, 80 (Laconia), 338: 68 (Thessaly), 403: 24 (Rhodes).
LH IIIA1.

93-553. Shallow cup. Fig. 28c, Pl. 22a

H. 0.033m; D. 0.10m (?).
Broken, restored, complete except for the greater part of the ring handle. Pinkish clay, buff slip, black paint almost entirely worn off. Shallow bowl with a broad, horizontal lip; high-swung ring handle; base raised concave. Monochrome.
FS 237-238.
Cf. examples listed by Furumark, *op. cit.*, pl. 133; Papadopoulos, *op. cit.*, figs. 180-181, 270; Giannopoulos 2008, pl. 54: 1-2; Mountjoy, *MDP*, fig. 52; *RMDP*, figs. 85: 45-47 (Laconia), 133: 48, 49 (Elis).
LH IIIA1.

94-564. One-handled carinated kylix. Fig. 30a, Pl. 22b

H. 0.099m; D. rim 0.012m.
Restored from seven fragments with a small part of rim missing. Pinkish clay, unpainted. Carinated bowl, short spreading lip, flattened handle from rim to bowl, its lower end being attached to the conical part of the bowl; straight-sided stem, disc base slightly convex.
FS 267.
Cf. examples listed by Furumark, *op. cit.*, pl. 146; Papadopoulos, *op. cit.*, figs. 179d, 269b; Stubbings, *Attica*, type H, fig. 10; Blegen, *PN I*, shape 27, figs. 331, 334, 336, 340, 343, 359; Benzi, *RCM*, pl. 174: e, h (Rhodes); Mountjoy, *RMDP*, fig. 91: 130, 131 (Laconia).
LH IIIA2.

95-565. Squat stirrup jar. Fig. 21b, Pl. 22c-d

H. 0.085M; D. 0.129m.
Spout, base and a large part of body lost. Pinkish clay yellowish slip, dark-brown to black paint, partly worn off. Perked-up squat globular body, convex top disc, narrow strap handles. Concentric circles on top disc, handles painted solid except for a reserved triangle next to the top disc; encircling loop at base of spout and false neck. Groups of bands and fine lines on body to line of spout attachment; sea- anemone on shoulder zone.
FS 180, ΓM 27: (?).
Cf. examples listed by Furumark, *op. cit.*, pl. 104; Papadopoulos, *Aigion*, pl. 30, 37, 50, 51, 59, 91, 92, 96; Mountjoy, *op. cit.*, figs. 70: 130 (Korinthia), 259: 160 (Boeotia), 272: 59, 60 (Euboea).
LH IIIB1.

96-566. Squat stirrup jar. Fig. 30c, Pl. 23a-b.

H. 0.10m; D. 0.129m.
Restored from many pieces; parts of body and one handle missing. Buff clay and slip, brown paint partly worn off. Squat globular shape, concave false neck with convex top disc, tubular lipped spout leaning outwards, narrow flattened handles, wide, low ring base. Base and outside of handles painted solid except for a reserved triangle next to the top disc; concentric circles with central dot on top disc. Groups of bands and fine lines on body to line of spout attachment; lip of spout painted solid, encircling loop at base of spout and false neck. Mycenaean flower on shoulder zone.
FS 178; FM 18: 100 (?).

Cf. examples listed by Furumark, *op. cit.*, pls. 102, 103; Papadopoulos, *Aigion*, pls. 26, 34, 76, 79, 76, 80, 94, 98; Mountjoy, *RMDP*, figs. 28: 190, 191 (Argolid), 60: 114 (Korinthia), 114: 72 (Messenia), 132: 44 (Elis), 189: 153 (Attica), 292: 50 (Phocis), 406: 40 (Rhodes), 444: 27 (Kos).
LH IIIA2.

97-567. Depressed globular stirrup jar. Fig. 31a, Pl. 23c

H. 0.103m; D. 0.118m.
Restored from many pieces; almost half of the body lost. Buff clay and slip, dark-brown to black paint, mostly worn off. Depressed globular body, vertical spout with splaying lip, narrow flattened handles, very low, hardly visible ring base. Concentric circles with central dot on top disc, base and handles painted solid except for a reserved triangle next to the top disc; separate rings on the rim of spout, at base of spout and the false neck. Groups of bands and fine lines on body; Mycenaean flower on shoulder zone.
FS 171; FM 18: 112.
Cf. examples listed by Furumark, *MP III*, 97; Mountjoy, *MDP*, fig. 93; *RMDP*, figs. 27: 188, 189 (Argolid), 69: 113 (Korinthia), 88: 94-96 (Laconia), 114: 71 (Messenia), 132: 42-43 (Elis), 143: 30 (Achaea), 161: 5-6 (Kephallenia), 189: 150-152 (Attica), 253: 86-88 (Boeotia), 272: 50-51 (Euboea), 292: 48-49 (Phocis), 339: 76-77 (Thessaly), 406: 39 (Rhodes), 444: 25-26 (Kos).
LH IIIA2.

98-568. Squat globular stirrup jar. Fig. 31b, Pl.23d

H. 0.088m; D. 0.127m.
Restored from many pieces with parts of body missing. Reddish-buff clay, yellowish slip, brown paint, partly worn off. Squat globular shape, flat top disc, tubular spout slightly leaning outwards, flattened handles, raised flat base. Base and outside of handles painted solid except for a reserved triangle next to the top disc; concentric circles on top disc. Rim of spout painted solid, encircling loop at base of spout and the false neck. Groups of bands and fine lines on body; multiple stem on shoulder zone.
FS 180; FM 19: 31.
Cf. examples listed by Furumark, *op. cit.*, pl. 104; for references, see No. 95-565.
LH IIIA2.

99-569. Fragmentary globular stirrup jar (?). Fig. 27a, Pl. 7a

Pres. H. 0.097m; D. 0.11m.
Five joining fragments preserve half of the body and base. Pinkish clay, yellowish slip, dark-brown paint partly worn off. Traces of ring around the base of false neck; shoulder left unpainted, groups of bands and fine lines on the body and the ring base.
FS 171.
Cf. Papadopoulos, *Mycenaean Achaea*, 75 (6 vases with undecorated shoulder: PM 215, 428, 625, 670, 898, BE 431); Mountjoy, *RMDP*, figs. 47: 357 (Tiryns), 54: 408 (Asine), 96: 189 (Ayios Stefanos), Giannopoulos 2008, pl. 25: 37, 69: 2 (Spaliareika).
LH IIIA2/B1.

Pottery sherds with no inventory numbers

100-? Fragment of squat globular stirrup jar (?). Fig. 31c, Pl. 24a

Dim. 0.073 x 0.027m.
Fragment of shoulder of a squat globular stirrup jar (?), decorated with a broad band and group of fine lines.
FS 178 (?).
LH IIIA2 (?).

101-? Belly fragments of a large piriform jar (?). Fig. 32A, Pls.

Dim. 0.18 x 0.17m.
Eleven joining belly fragments of a large three-handled piriform jar (?), decorated with a group of three wide bands.
FS 34 or 35 (?).
LH IIIA2 Early (?).

102-? Belly and shoulder fragments of a large piriform jar (?). Fig. 32a, Pl. 24b

Dim. 0.21 x 0.14m.
Five joining belly and shoulder fragments of a vase similar to the preceding shape (**101-?**), decorated with a group of three wide bands framed by bivalve shells.
FS 34-35; FM 25: 9.
Cf. examples listed by Furumark, *MP III*, pls. 23-25; Papadopoulos, *Aigion*, pls. 48, 60; Karantzali 2001, 45-47, figs. 35-38, pls. 33-36 (Pylona-Rhodes); Nikolentzos 2011, pls. 74-76 (Elis).
LH IIIA2.

103-? Belly and shoulder fragments of a large piriform jar (?). Fig. 32c, Pl. 25a

Dim. 0.245 x 0.14m.
Three joining belly and shoulder fragments of a jar similar to Nos. 102-103, decorated with a group of three wide bands, concentric arcs and accessorial sea-anemone motifs.
FS 34-35; FM 44: 3; 27: 17.
For references, see No. 102.
LH IIIA2.

104-? Stem and lower part of bowl of a kylix. Fig. 33a, Pl. 24a

Pres. H. 0.052m.
The greater upper part of cylindrical stem and small part of the lower part of bowl of a high-stemmed (?) kylix. Reddish-buff clay, unpainted.
FS 256-257 (?).
LH IIIA2 (?).

105-? Kylix. Fig. 33b

H. 0.15m, D. rim 0.172m.
Complete. Yellow-buff clay with smooth surface. Unpainted. Deep conical bowl, lipless; narrow cylindrical stem slightly tapering downwards. Convex base hollowed by a small cavity corresponding to diameter of stem. Two vertical round handles from rim to high up on the side of the bowl.
FS 274.
LH IIIB1.

106-? Fragmentary kylix (?). Fig. 34c, Pl. 24c

Pres. H. 0.045m; D. rim 0.142m.
Upper part of the semi-globular bowl with a thickened lip and high-swung strap handle. Yellow-buff clay and slip. Unpainted.
FS 270 (?).
LH IIA (?).

107-? Fragment of bowl of a shallow cup (?). Fig. 34b, Pl. 25d

Dim. 0.03 x 0.025m.
Small fragment of shallow semi-globular cup with flaring rim decorated with spiral. Reddish-yellow clay and slip, red-brown paint.
FS 220 (?).
LH IIIA2 (?).

108-? Fragment of bowl of a spouted cup (?). Fig. 34a, Pl. 25d

Dim. 0.043 x 0.065m.
Fragment of a deep, closing semi-globular spouted cup with a flaring lipless rim, decorated with a broad band below it. Pinkish-buff clay and slip, brown paint.
FS 249 (?).
LH IIIB1 (?).

109-? Fragment of a large piriform jar (?). Fig. 35a, Pl. 25b

Dim. 0.0104 x 0.185m.
Lower shoulder fragment of a large piriform jar, decorated with three horizontal bands. Pinkish-buff clay and slip, red-brown paint.
FS 34 (?).
LH IIIA2 (?).

110-? Fragment of a large piriform jar (?). Fig. 28b, Pl. 24a

Dim. 0.067 x 0.081m.
Shoulder part with the spring of a handle of a large piriform jar, decorated with concentric arcs (?). Pinkish-buff clay and slip, red-brown paint.
FS 34 (?).
For references, see No. 102.
LH IIIA2 (?).

111-? Fragment with pictorial decoration. Fig. 35C, Pl. 25c

Dim. 0.04 x 0.037m.
Shoulder and belly part of a stemmed krater (?) decorated with a pictorial design of a man behind an animal of unknown kind. Pinkish clay, yellowish slip, dark-brown paint.
FS 7-8 (?).
LH IIIA2 Late (?).

COMMENTARY ON THE FINDS

I. *The Mycenaean pottery*

The Mycenaean pottery found in the four chamber tombs excavated by Mastrokostas, apart from an unknown number of potsherds (14 counted and included in this catalogue), amounted to 39 complete and 40 more or less fragmentary vases of perhaps 14 basic shapes.

The number of vases in each tomb ranges from 9 vases in tomb B, to 33 in tomb D. All vases were found empty, and as regards their probable use, fabric and technique, what has been suggested and said for those found in our excavation at the cemetery in 1970 is also valid for these pots, and there is no need to repeat them here. As to typology, 14 forms are represented. Two more or less unique shapes (Nos. 16-486 and 70-428) are not found exactly in Furumark.

By far the commonest shapes are the stirrup jar, amphoriskos and piriform jar, comprising 39, 10 and 8 examples respectively. For the rest, the globular jug, the rounded and straight-sided alabastron and the kylix are relatively frequent – 5 to 7 specimens – while none of the other shapes is represented by more than 3 vases.

A. CLOSED SHAPES

1. Stirrup jar

Type 167
Piriform heavy or conical.
Nos. 1-414, 13-483, 82-440, 83-441 (4 examples).
LH IIIB1.

Type 171
Globular with height almost equal to diameter.
Nos. 10-445, 73-431, 78-436, 85-443, 97-567, 99-569 (6 examples).
LH IIIA: 2b (-B).

Type 173
Globular with height greater than diameter.
Nos. 11-446, 12-447, 14-484, 79-437, 80-438, 81-439, 88-489 (?) (8 examples).
LH IIIB1.

Type 175
Globular with height greater than diameter.
Nos. 2-415, 4-417, 25-387, 37-389, 38-390, 51-479, 52-480 (7 examples).
LH IIIC.

Type 176
Globular with height greater than diameter.
Nos. 18-548, 26-388 (?), 39-391, 49-477, 55-399, 72-430, (6 examples).
LH IIIC.

Type 178
Squat globular-biconical with diameter greater than height.
Nos. 96-566, 100-? (2 examples).
LH IIIA2.

Type 180
Perked-up, squat globular.
Nos. 36-385, 74-432, 95-565, 98-568 (4 examples).
LH IIIB1.

Type 182
Conical or conical-piriform.
Nos. 15-485, 56-400 (2 examples).
LH IIIB1.

Type 184
Cylindrical.
No. 16-486 (1 example).
LH IIIB2.

The stirrup jar, represented by 39 specimens, as in other Achaean Mycenaean cemeteries, is the most common shape in the Aigion tombs excavated by Mastrokostas.[4] Five main varieties of shape occur: globular, squat, piriform, conical and cylindrical – the globular greatly outnumbering all other varieties with 26 finds. Almost all vases are typical forms with parallels from elsewhere in Greece. The 4 piriform specimens, with their heavy or conical form, are interesting, and although finding some parallels in other regions, the type has not previously been noted and remains rare in Achaea. The single cylindrical find is another interesting specimen because of the peculiarity in the Mycenaean repertory of Achaea and the rarity of the type elsewhere in Greece.

---

[4] Cf. Papadopoulos, *Mycenaean Achaea*, 71, and *Aigion*, 39.

Decoration of these vases consists of floral and other abstract motifs on the shoulder, similar to those known from other sites and deliberate alteration of bands and fine lines on the body. What is of special interest is the frequency of a subsidiary decorated zone below the shoulder (11 examples)[5] and the painting underneath the base, either with concentric circles (1 example) or a cross (2 examples).[6] The shoulder of one vase only is left undecorated. Chronologically they range from LH IIIA2 to LH IIIC, although most of them belong to the LH IIIB period.

2. Piriform jar

Type 34-35 (?)
Uncertain shape (large piriform with three vertical handles).
Nos. 32-496, 91-492, 101-?, 102-?, 103-?, 109-?, 110-? (7 examples).
LH IIIA-B.

Type 31
Piriform with three vertical handles.
No. 23-397 (1 example).
LH IIIA1.

The shape is represented by a single complete specimen and 7 catalogued fragments. The single complete vase No. 23-397 of FS 31 has three vertical handles, typical diaper net decoration on shoulder and groups of bands and lines below and on its lower body are painted solid. It is dated to the LH IIIA1 period.[7] For the 7 fragmentary specimens it is not altogether clear which FS group is most applicable, particularly as most of the bodies of all the finds are missing. However, judging by their size and decoration (bands, plastic knobs and characteristic 'Palace-Style' motifs reminiscent of large jar BE 673 (found in 1970 in tomb 5) and some similar fragments from other tombs of this cemetery,[8] they should almost certainly be assigned to FS types 34-35 and to LH IIIA-B date. The shape occurs more frequently on Rhodes than in other Mycenaean regions, and this led Stubbings, Taylour and Papadopoulos[9] to suggest Rhodian origin and production. However, after the analysis of some examples from Ialysos[10] and Aigion,[11] which revealed that they were imported from the Argolid, this theory is no longer valid.

---

[5] In contrast to those discovered in 1970 (one example only).
[6] Cf. Papadopoulos, *Mycenaean Achaea,* 80.
[7] Cf. French, *BSA* 59 (1964), 244, fig. 1: 6.
[8] Papadopoulos, *Aigion,* pls. 48, 10b; Karantzali 2001, pls. 33-36; Nikolentzos 2011, pls. 74-76 (Elis).
[9] *Attica,* 14, *MPI,* 128, *Aigion,* 18, 40.
[10] Jones and Mee, 'Spectographic Analyses of Mycenaean Pottery from Ialysos on Rhodes. Results and Implications', *JFA* 5 (1978), 461-470.
[11] Papadopoulos and Jones, 'Rhodiaka in Achaea', *OpAth* XIII: 15 (1980), 225-235.

3. Rounded alabastron

Type 84
No. 92-552 (1 example).
LH IIIA1.

Type 85
Nos. 17-487, 35-384 (?), 57-401, 86-444 (4 examples).
LH IIIB-C, LH IIIA1-2, LH IIIA2, LH IIIA2/B1.

There are 2 complete specimens (Nos. 17-487 and 92-552) and 3 fragmentary ones (Nos. 35-384, 57-401, 86-444). Of the 2 complete specimens, No. 92-552, of the flat variety and with its fine decoration of rock-pattern and sea-anemone on the shoulder, bands and fine lines on the lower body and concentric circles on the base, is one of the best examples in the Aigion repertory, with parallels from other sites; it seems to be the earliest of the 5 examples and is dated to LH IIIA1. The second complete two-handled alabastron of the round variety (No. 17-487), which is decorated with a fringed band on the shoulder, bands on the lower body and concentric circles on base, could be the latest, assigned to the LH IIIB-C period. The fragmentary examples have lost their handles and part of the neck (No. 57-401), or large parts of body and neck (No. 86-444), or even more than half of the body, neck and rim (No. 35-384). However, even though the decoration of No. 35-384 is mostly worn off, on the basis of their preserved profile they may be assigned to FS 85. Moreover, in conjunction with the decoration of No. 57-40 (rock-pattern) and No. 86-444 (multiple stem), as well as parallels from elsewhere and their context, it is possible to date them between LH IIIA1-2 and LH IIIA2/B1.

4. Square-sided alabastron

Type 96
Nos. 20-550, 41-393, 42-394, 64-422, 69-427 (5 examples).
LH IIIC Early.

Type 97
Based
No. 70-428 (1 example).
LH IIIC Early.

Type 98
Side-handled, height greater than diameter.
No. 58-402 (1 example).
LH IIIC Late.

Of the 7 examples found in these tombs, 3 are complete and intact (Nos. 20-550, 42-394, 70-428), with the remaining 4 being more or less well preserved, with some cracking, chipping and rubbing of surfaces. Straight lower body, splaying or spreading neck, bottom flat or convex. No. 70-428 has a low ring base and is the first to be found and known so far in Achaea. It may be an import from the Dodecanese, where the form is more frequent.[12] Two opposite horizontal handles on the shoulder placed in line with the sides at the angle between the upper and the lower part of the body, usually turned slightly outwards. They are carefully shaped and finely decorated, either all over with bands and lines (Nos. 42-394, 64-422) or with bands on the body and several designs on the shoulder zone (chain of lozenges: No. 20-550; running spirals: No. 41-393; foliate band: No. 69-427; parallel chevrons: No. 70-428). Especially interesting and unique is the decoration of No. 58-402, with a chain of lozenges on the shoulder and panelled patterns framed by two bands on the lower body consisting of antithetic spiral, zig-zag and concentric semicircles on the front and antithetic spiral and fringed chequers on the back. Such panelled patterns are usual on kraters and deep bowls, but they are quite unknown on alabastra elsewhere in Greece. The neck is painted solid or banded; handles painted solid, barred or with splash(es), concentric circles underneath the base of Nos. 64-422 and 20-550 (?). Chronologically, all examples are dated to LH IIIC Early, the only exception being No. 58-402, which is later (LH IIIC Late).

5. Amphoriskos

Type 59
Globular shape, short flaring neck, lipless rim; two round horizontal handles.
Nos. 30-494, 48-476, 54-398, 61-419, 62-420, 63-421, 68-426, 75-433, 76-434, 77-435 (10 examples).
LH IIIC.

The shape, second in frequency, after the stirrup jar, is represented by 3 complete and intact (Nos. 30-494, 54-398, 62-420) and 7 more or less fragmentary examples. There are minor variations in shape, ranging from globular to globular ovoid or baggy and dumpy-baggy, but common to them all are the wide, low neck and the two round handles placed on the belly or high up on the shoulder. Only one vase (No. 54-398) is painted monochrome, while decoration on another (No. 61-419) is too worn to be traceable. Necks and mouths are painted inside and out, or painted outside only (No. 68-426), or painted inside and the exterior left blank (No. 48-476) or painted outside and banded inside (No. 76-434). The

---

[12] Cf. examples listed by Furumark, *MP III*, pl. 55 (97:4), Morricone, figs. 72: 25, 175: 128, 263: 217, 297: 254 (Kos-Langada); Mountjoy, *RMDP*, 1099 ('The based FS 97, a Dodecanesian type which is rare on the Mainland'), fig. 450: 77.

rim of one specimen is dotted (No. 76-434), the base of another (No. 62-420) has concentric circles underneath and the handles are mostly painted solid or barred. Decoration on the shoulder has a fairly limited range of motifs, i.e. simple and double horizontal zig-zag, simple or double wavy line, scale pattern, multiple stem, and in one instance (No. 48-476) two different designs (wavy line and lozenge) are used one on either side, which is exceptional and unique in the cemetery of Aigion.[13]

Chronologically the shape is confined to the LH IIIC period, throughout which (Early, Middle, Late) it seems to persist.

6. Globular Jug

Type 111
No. 47-475 (1 example).
LH IIIC Late.

Type 112
No. 40-392 (1 example).
LH IIIA2 Early.

Type 113
Nos. 66-424, 67-425 (2 examples).
LH IIIA2.

Type 114
Nos. 19-549, 50-478 (2 examples).
LH IIIA2 (B).

Type 115
No. 31-495 (1 example).
LH IIIC Middle.

The shape is represented by five complete (Nos. 19-549, 40-392, 47-475, 66-424, 67-425) and two fragmentary (Nos. 57-401, 86-444) specimens. They are much like those known from most Mycenaean sites, especially Kephallenia, and correspond more or less to Furumark types 111-115, with minor variations in the details, and in contrast to those from Kephallenia none of them is handmade. As regards their decoration, 3 vases are monochrome (Nos. 40-392, 47-475, 66-424), 2 are banded all over (Nos. 19-549, 67-425), and 2 are banded on the neck and body and bear different motifs on the shoulder (radiated vertical bands: 31-495;

---

[13] Cf. Iakovides, *Perati B'*, fig. 78: 123.

two horizontal zones of dots 50-478). Chronologically, 5 specimens belong to LH IIIA2 Early or Late, and the other two could be assigned to LH IIIC Middle and Late.

7. Lekythos

Type 122
No. 29-493 (1 example).
LH IIIC Late.

Type 123
No. 33-383 (1 example).
LH IIIC Late.

Of the two examples found in the cemetery, the first is fragmentary but mended and the second is complete. Globular body with the vertical handle extending either from the rim (No. 33-382) or below it (No. 29-493) to the shoulder. The first is most probably monochrome and the second is decorated with groups of bands on the body and concentric semicircles and groups of vertical wavy lines on the shoulder. Its decoration closely resembles that of some stirrup jars from elsewhere in Achaea.[14] They find parallels elsewhere in Greece[15] and both could be assigned to the LH IIIC Late period.

8. Askos

Type 194
No. 34-383 (1 example).
LH IIIA2.

Type 195
Nos. 71-429, 87-488 (2 examples).
LH IIIB/C Early, LH IIIB1.

All three examples are more or less fragmentary but restored. The baseless No. 34-383 is of the usual curved and crescent-like shape (Stubbings type B);[16] one end opens in a small mouth or spout, the other terminates almost in a point. It has a closed top or back surmounted by a flattened loop handle placed longitudinally. The two based askoi (Stubbings type A) are of globular (No. 87-488) or depressed globular (No. 71-429) shape with a tubular spout, flattened

---

[14] Cf. e.g. Papadopoulos, *Mycenaean Achaea,* fig. 214c
[15] *Op.cit.* p. 92
[16] *Attica,* 53, fig. 22

loop handle with both joints on top of the body in line with spout, and raised base. The baseless specimen is monochrome, and of the two based finds, both of which are ornamented with broad stripes around the body and on the neck and handle, No. 71-429 is decorated on the shoulder with a single horizontal wavy line and No. 87-488 with a lozenge.

The askos, a rare shape in Mycenaean contexts[17] but less so in Achaea, is represented in the Aigion cemetery by both baseless and based variants. The baseless specimen which finds parallels elsewhere[18] is undoubtedly an imitation of a goatskin,[19] while the two based examples have much in common with other askoi from other sites.[20] Chronologically the baseless specimen (No. 34-383) is earlier (LH IIIA2) than the two based finds, which could be assigned to LH IIIB1 (No. 87-488) and LH IIIB/C Early (No. 71-429) periods.

B. OPEN SHAPES

9. Krater (?)

Type 7-8 (?)
111-? (1 example).
LH IIIA2 Late.

Only a fragment from shoulder and belly survives, so its exact shape is not determinable. It may belong to a stemmed krater, and this is strengthened by its pictorial decoration consisting of a man behind an animal of unknown kind. The krater, often the vehicle for pictorial decoration, was entirely unknown in Achaea until 1970,[21] in contrast with other areas, such as the Argolid, Rhodes and Cyprus,[22] where it was more common. Chronologically, No. 111-? may be dated to the LH IIIA2 Late period.

10. Stemmed bowl (?)

Type 304 (?)
No. 89-490 (1 example).
LH IIIA2 Late.

---

[17] It survives, however, until the very late Mycenaean period, Cf. e.g. *AE* (1933), 82, fig. 27a.4, Metaxata-Kephallenia, (1932) 120, pl.8: 120 (Lakkithra).
[18] See examples listed by Furumark, *MP*, 617, and Papadopoulos, *Mycenaean Achaea*, 101, n. 50.
[19] Cf. Iakovidis, *Perati B*, 251.
[20] Cf. examples listed by Papadopoulos, *op. cit.,* 101, n. 54,
[21] When the first specimen was found in our excavation at this cemetery, *Aigion*, 42, pl. 18b (BE 606).
[22] Cf. examples listed by Furumark, *MP*, 586.

One fragmentary example, in pinkish undecorated ware, probably belongs to FS 304. The shape known from other sites appears in LH IIIA and occurs throughout the succeeding LH IIIB and LH IIIC periods.[23] Our specimen could be assigned to LH IIIA 2 Late.[24]

11. Kylix

Type 256-7
104-? (1 example).
LH IIIA2 (?)

Type 265
No. 22-396 (1 example).
LH IIIA2 Late.

Type 267
No. 94-564 (1 example).
LH IIIA2.

Type 271 (?)
No. 60-418 (1 example).
LH IIB.

Type 270 (?)
No. 106-? (1 example).
LH IIA (?).

Type 274
No. 105-? (1 example).
LH IIIB1.

Kylix is one of the frequent shapes in this cemetery, accounting for six examples, of which only one was complete (No. 105-?) and another was restored to give a complete profile (No. 22-396). Two kylikes have lost part of the wall (No. 60-418) and rim (No. 94-564), while in two other examples the upper part of stem and lower bowl (No. 104-?) and the upper part of bowl and the high-swung handle (No. 106-?) survive.

It must be noted, therefore, that assignment to the types listed above – with the exception of the two complete specimens – is tentative and by no means

---

[23] Cf. Stubbings, *Attica,* 39.
[24] Cf. examples listed by Furumark, *MP,* 638; Mountjoy, *MDP,* fig. 112.

definite. Two kylikes are painted monochrome (Nos. 22-396 and 60-418) and the remaining four are left plain.

The presence of two low-stemmed examples (No. 60-418 and possibly No. 106-?) is interesting as it shows the evolution from the LH II 'Ephyrean' goblet to the LH III kylix. Chronologically these two kylikes seem to be earlier (LH II A-B) than the four others, which could be assigned to the LH IIIA2 and B1 periods.

12. Shallow cup

Type 237-8
No. 93-553 (1 example).
LH IIIA1.

Type 220 (?)
No. 107-? (1 example).
LH IIIA2 (?).

The shallow cup is a common Mycenaean pottery shape. The fragmentary but restored and almost complete monochrome cup No. 93-553, with a flat rim and a high-swung ring handle certainly imitates a metallic form.[25] The exact shape to which the small fragment No. 107-? belongs is not determinable, but it is possible, on the basis of its profile and the spiral decoration, to assign it to FS 220.[26]

Shallow cups persist throughout the Late Mycenaean period. Chronologically, our first example seems to be earlier (LH IIIA1) than the second, which could be cautiously assigned to the LH IIIA2 period.

13. Spouted deep cup

Type 249 (?)
No. 108-? (1 example).
LH IIIB1 (?).

Assignment of this fragmentary piece to FS 249 and to the LH IIIB1 period is very tentative and by no means definite. The shape, which is the second most common in Achaea, after the bell type,[27] betrays a metallic origin, although no actual metal spouted cup is known to the present authors.

---

[25] Cf. Evans, *PM II:2*, 637; Stubbings, *Attica*, 63; Furumark, *MP*, 52,56; Persson, *NTD*, 135; Papadopoulos, *Mycenaean Achaea*, 120.
[26] Cf. Mountjoy, *MDP*, fig. 100: 2, 4.
[27] Papadopoulos, *Mycenaean Achaea*, 123, fig. 273E-f.

14. Throne model

No. 24-386 (1 example).

Clay model of a tripod throne, complete. It is the only throne without occupant (empty) found so far in the region of Achaea. It belongs to Mylonas type B[28] and its decoration is simple, consisting of horizontal and vertical stripes and rows of dashes. It has been suggested that throne models are associated with representations of seated deities, commonly found in the Aegean iconography.[29] They occur either individually, like our example, or together with seated female figurines of the well- known *Phi* and *Psi* types. It is dated to the LH IIIA period.

C. Other finds

As with the other tombs excavated in 1970, the rarity of metallic objects is observable in these tombs. Only two plain round rings were found, one gold (No. 8-407) and the other bronze (No. 45-412); other finds included a fragmentary pair of depilatory tweezers (No. 9-408) and a bronze fibula of the violin-bow type (No. 46-413), whose upper surface (the leaf-shaped bow) is decorated with four plastic dots set in a cross-rhomboid arrangement. There were only two glass beads, one seed-shaped (No. 7-406) and the other globular (No. 27-409), and 29 buttons of different material and shape, i.e. 5 made of clay (4 biconical, 1 conical) and 24 of black, purple, pale-green, greyish-green steatite (19 conical, 5 shanked). All are plain and without decoration.

---

[28] For references see above in the Catalogue under No. 24.
[29] Cf. Mylonas, see above notes for No. 24, and Divari-Valakou, in *Troy, Mycenae, Tiryns, Orchomenos*, 373.

GENERAL COMMENTS AND CONCLUSIONS

The following main points and tentative conclusions emerge from the present study. As stated above, the material from the 4 chamber tombs excavated in 1967 is, when compared with that from the 11 tombs excavated in 1970, much greater in number (111 compared to 73), indicating richer burials; the finds however were roughly of the same variety of pottery shapes (14 and 16 respectively). Again, by far the commonest shape is the stirrup jar, comprising 39 examples, followed by the amphoriskos (10 specimens). Other common shapes are the piriform jar (8 examples), the globular jug and the straight-sided alabastron (7 vases each), the kylix and the rounded alabastron (6 and 5 examples respectively), while none of the other shapes is represented by more than three pots.

It has been suggested[30] that among the material from the region of Aigion, which is stylistically different from and generally earlier than that of western Achaea, are the tall conical-piriform stirrup jars, some with an unusually wide base, (FS 167), which are rarely found in other western Mycenaean sites,[31] but they are more frequent in the Argolid (Petsas House), Boeotia, Rhodes and Cyprus.[32] Noteworthy also is the occurrence of the cylindrical stirrup jar No. 16-486, which is of almost the same shape and proportions as the one found earlier in the same region and first published by Aström,[33] and two others from Leontion tomb III.[34] The presence of these two vases is important since the shape is generally very rare.[35] Also, the occurrence of 3 based vases (1 straight-sided alabastron (No. 70-428) and 2 askoi (Nos. 71-429, 87-488)) is interesting, possibly indicating a local preference or influence from elsewhere (i.e. the Dodecanese).[36] Another interesting feature is the relative frequency of some other shapes, such as the amphoriskos, piriform jar and globular jug, which are all rare in the tombs excavated in 1970, while there is no terracotta figurine of

---

[30] Cf. Papadopoulos, *Mycenaean Achaea*, 80
[31] E.g. in Elis, Messenia and Aetoloacarnania.
[32] Cf. French, *BSA* 60 (1965) 193; Symeonoglou, *Kadmeia I*, 26,32; Stubbings, *MPL*, 69; Papadopoulos, *Mycenaean Achaea*, 80; Benzi, *RCM*, 74, *CVA, BM.1*, pls. 2-3 (Cyprus).
[33] *OpAth* 5 (1965) 91, fig. 1: 1-3.
[34] Cf. Giannopoulos, 2008, 152, Taf. 65: 6-7.
[35] Furumark (*MP,* 45, n. 6, and p. 615) mentions a few specimens from mainland Greece. For additional references, see Papadopoulos, *Mycenaean Achaea,* 80 (from Cyprus, Crete, Kos and Perati).
[36] Many such vases have been found in Kos-Langada and Rhodes, cf. Morricone, figs. 72: 25, 175ö 128, 263: 217, 297: 254; *CVA. D,* pl. 46: 5. Also Benzi, *RCM*, 70-75, and Mountjoy, *RMDP,* 1038, 1099, fig. 425: 168-170 ('The based FS 97 is popular in the Dodecanese' and 'The based FS 97, a Dodecanesian type which is rare on the Mainland').

any type and the throne model (latticed or open without occupant) is so far a unique find in Achaea.

As regards decoration, only five vases are unpainted and a few are monochrome; all others are decorated with usual Mycenaean designs. Unique are the pictorial decoration of a man behind an animal (No. 111-?) and the painting of the cylindrical body of the straight-sided alabastron (No. 58-402), with two different panelled patterns. It is notable, too, the relative frequency of body zones on stirrup jars, which probably betrays some trends of local style, and the relief decoration of plastic knobs on some sherds belonging to large piriform jars, similar to those found in 1970, indicating contacts with the Dodecanese.[37]

The rarity of small finds is surprising – as with the tombs excavated in 1970. These included two simple rings (one bronze, one gold), a pair of bronze depilatory tweezers, three glass beads and a small number of buttons, and this may be explained as a feature of the local burial habits.

Chronologically, the time-span of the use of the four tombs excavated by Mastrokostas in 1967 extends from LH II A(?)-B, up to and including the whole of LH IIIC, with its greatest prosperity during the LH IIIA and B periods. In this way it seems to conform to and strengthen the evidence provided by the eleven tombs of the same cemetery excavated by Papadopoulos in 1970.[38]

---

[37] Cf. Papadopoulos, *Aigion*, 40, 46, pls. 48,60; Papadopoulos-Jones, 'Rhodiaka in Achaea', *OpAth* XIII: 15 (1980), 225-235. Also Karantzali, 2001, 45-47, figs. 35-38 (Asprospilia tombs, Rhodes); Nikilentzos, 2011, 221 ff.
[38] Papadopoulos, *op. cit.*, 46.

ABBREVIATIONS

I. For Periodicals and Series

AAA Athens Annals of Archaeology

ADelt Archaiologikon Deltion

AM Mitteilungen des deutschen archäologischen Instituts: athenische Abteilung

Annuario Annuario della scuola italiana di Atene e delle missioni italiani in oriente

BSA Annual of the British School at Athens

JFA Journal of Field Archaeology

OpAth Opuscula Atheniensia

PAE Praktika tis Archaeologikis Etaireias

BAR British Archaeological Reports

PBF Prähistorische Bronzefunde

SIMA Studies in Mediterranean Archaeology

II. Special Abbreviations

Aigion Papadopoulos, A.J. *Excavations at Aigion-1970* (SIMA 46), Göteborg, 1976.

Attica Stubbings, F.H. 'The Mycenaean Pottery of Attica', *BSA* 42, 1947, 1-75.

Brodbeck-Jucker Brodbeck-Jucker, S. *Mykenische Funde von Kephallenia in archäologischen Museum Neuchâtel,* Rome 1986.

CMP Furumark, A. *The Chronology of Mycenaean Pottery,* Stockholm 1941.

Giannopoulos 2008 Giannopoulos, T.G. *Die letzte Elite der mykenischen Welt. Achaia in mykenischer Zeit und das Phenomen der Kriegerbestattungen im 12-11 Jahrhundert von Chr.* Bonn 2008.

***Fibeln* I** Kilian, K. *Fibeln in Thessalien vor der mykenischer bis zur archaischen Zeit* (PBF XIV.2), München 1975.

***Fibeln* II** Sapouna-Sakellarakis, E. *Die Fibeln der griechischen Inseln* (PBF XIV.4), München 1978.

Fibules Blinkenberg, C. *Fibules greques et orientales* (Lindiaka V), Copenhagen, 1926.

GRJ Higgins, R.A. *Greek and Roman Jewellery*, London 1961.

***Kadmeia* I** Symeonoglou, S. *Kadmeia I. Mycenaean Finds from Thebes, Greece. Excavation at 14 Oedipus St.* (SIMA 35), Göteborg 1973.

MDP Mountjoy, P.A. *Mycenaean Decorated Pottery. A Guide to Identification* (SIMA 73), Göteborg 1986.

Morricone Morricone, L. 'Eleona e Langada, sepolchreti della tarda Eta del Bronzo a Coo', *Annuario* 43-44 (1965-66) 5-616.

MPI Taylour, L.W. *Mycenaean Pottery in Italy and Adjacent Areas*, Cambridge 1958.

MP III Aström, P., *et al.* (eds.). Furumark, A. *Mycenaean Pottery III, Plates*, Stockholm 1992.

Mycenaean Achaea Papadopoulos, T.J. *Mycenaean Achaea 1-2* (SIMA 55), Göteborg 1978/79

NTD Persson, A.W. *New Tombs at Dendra near Midea*, Lund 1942

PN Blegen, C.W., *et al. The Palace of Nestor at Pylos in Western Messenia I-III*, Princeton 1966-1973.

RCM Benzi, M. *Rodi e la Civiltà Micenea I-II*, Roma 1992.

RMDP Mountjoy, P.A. *Regional Mycenaean Decorated Pottery I-II*, Raden/Westf. 1999.

III. Descriptive terms used in the catalogue of finds

D. = Diameter

H. = Height

L. = Length

Dim. = Dimensions

Pres. H. = Preserved Height

Pres. L. = Preserved Length

FM = Furumark Motifs

FS = Furumark Shapes

BIBLIOGRAPHY

Aström, P., Hägg, R., Walberg, G. (eds) 1992. Furumark, A. *Mycenaean Pottery III, Plates*, Stockholm.
Benzi, M. 1992. *Rodi e la Civiltà Micenea, I-II*, Roma.
Blegen, C., et al. 1966-1973. *The Palace of Nestor at Pylos in Western Messenia, I-III*, Princeton.
Blinkenberg, C. 1926. *Fibules greques et orientales* (Lindiaka V), Copenhagen.
Brodbeck-Jucker, S. 1986. *Mykenische Funde von Kephallenia im archäologischen Museum Neuchâtel*, (Arcaeologica 42), Rome.
Divari-Valakou, N. 1990, in Demakopoulou K. (ed.), *Troy-Mycenae-Tiryns-Orchomenos*, Athens.
French, E. 1967. Pottery from Late Helladic iiib 1 Destruction Contexts at Mycenae, *BSA* 62, 149-193.
French, E. 1971. The Development of Mycenaean Terracotta Figurines, *BSA* 66, 101-187.
Furumark, A. 1941. *The Mycenaean Pottery. Analysis and Classification*, Stockholm.
Furumark, A. 1941. *The Chronology of Mycenaean Pottery*, Stockholm.
Giannopoulos, Th. 2008. *Die letzte Elite der mykenischen Welt. Achaia in mykenischer Zeit und das Phänomen der Kriegerbestattungen Im 12-11 Jahrhundert von Chr*, Bonn.
Higgins, R.A. 1961. *Greek and Roman Jewellery*, London.
Iakovidis, S.E. 1970. *Perati. To Nekrotapheion Α-Γ*, Athens.
Kanta, A. 2008. *The Late Minoan III Period in Crete. A Survey of Sites, Pottery and their Distribution* (SIMA 58), Göteborg.
Karantzali, E. 2001. *The Mycenaean Cemetery at Pylona on Rhodes* (BAR, International Series 988), Oxford.
Kilian, K. 1975. *Fibeln in Thessalien vor der mykenischen bis zur archaischen Zeit* (PBF. XIV.2), München.
Kontorli-Papadopoulou, L. 2003. Late Mycenaean Achaean Vases and Bronzes in Berlin, *AM* 118, 23-47, pls. 6-16.
Kyparissis, N. 1939. Ανασκαφαί εν Αρχαία Αχαϊα, *PAE*, 103 ff.
Morricone, L. 1965-1966. Eleona e Langada, sepolchreti della tarda Eta del Bronzo a Coo, *Annuario*, 27-28, 5-616.
Mountjoy, P.A. 1986. *Mycenaean Decorated Pottery. A Guide to Identification* (SIMA 73), Göteborg.
Mountjoy, P.A. 1999. *Regional Mycenaean Decorated Pottery I-II*, Racden/Westf.
Mylonas, G.E. 1956. Seated and multiple Mycenaean figurines, in Weinberg S. (ed.), *The Aegean and the Near East, Studies presented to H. Goldman*, 117, New York.
Nikolentzos K. 2011, "Μυκηναϊκή Ηλεία: Πολιτιστική και Πολιτική Εξέλιξη. Εθνολογικά Δεδομένα και Προβλήματα", τ.Α-Β, Athens
Papadopoulos. A.J. 1976. *Excavations at Aigion-1970* (SIMA 46), Göteborg.

Papadopoulos, T.J. 1978/79. *Mycenaean Achaea I-II* (SIMA 55), Göteborg.
Papazoglou-Manioudaki, E. 1999. *Ο μυκηναϊκός οικισμός του Αιγίου και η πρώιμη μυκηναϊκή εποχή στην Αχαΐα*, (αδημ. διδ.διατριβή), Athens.
Paschalidis, K. 2014. *Το Μυκηναϊκό Νεκροταφείο του Κλάους-Πατρών*, (αδημ. διδ.διατριβή), *Ιωάννινα*.
Persson, A.W. 1942. *New Tombs at Dendra near Midea*, Lund.
Sapouna-Sakellarakis, E. 1978. *Die Fibeln der griechischen Inseln* (PBF XIV.4), München.
Stubbings, F.H. 1947. The Mycenaean Pottery of Attica, *BSA* 42, 1-75.
Symeonoglou, S. 1973. *Kadmeia I. Mycenaean Finds from Thebes, Greece. Excavation at 14 Oedipus St.* (SIMA 35), Göteborg.
Taylour, L.W. 1958. *Mycenaean Pottery in Italy and Adjacent Areas*, Cambridge.
Wardle, K. 1972. *The Greek Bronze Age West of the Pindus. A Study of the period ca. 3000-1000 B.C. in Epiros, Aetolo-Akarnania, the Ionian Islands and Albania with reference to the Aegean, Adriatic and Balkan Regions* (Unpublished Ph.D. thesis, London University).
Yalouris, N. 1954. Ανασκαφή εν Αιγίω, *PAE*, 287 ff.

PLATES AND FIGURES

PLATE 1. STIRRUP JARS NOS. 414, 415.

a

b

c

d

PLATE 2. STIRRUP JARS NOS. 417, 445, 446, 447.

PLATES AND FIGURES 63

a

b

c

d

PLATE 3. STIRRUP JARS NOS. 483, 484.

a

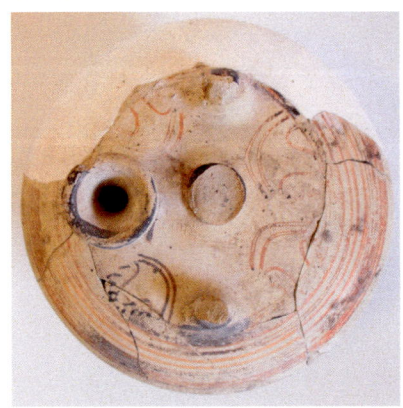

b

c

d

PLATE 4. STIRRUP JARS NOS. 485, 486; ROUNDED ALABSTRON NO. 487.

PLATE 5. STIRRUP JAR NO. 548; STRAIGHT-SIDED ALABASTRON NO. 550; KYLIX NO. 396.

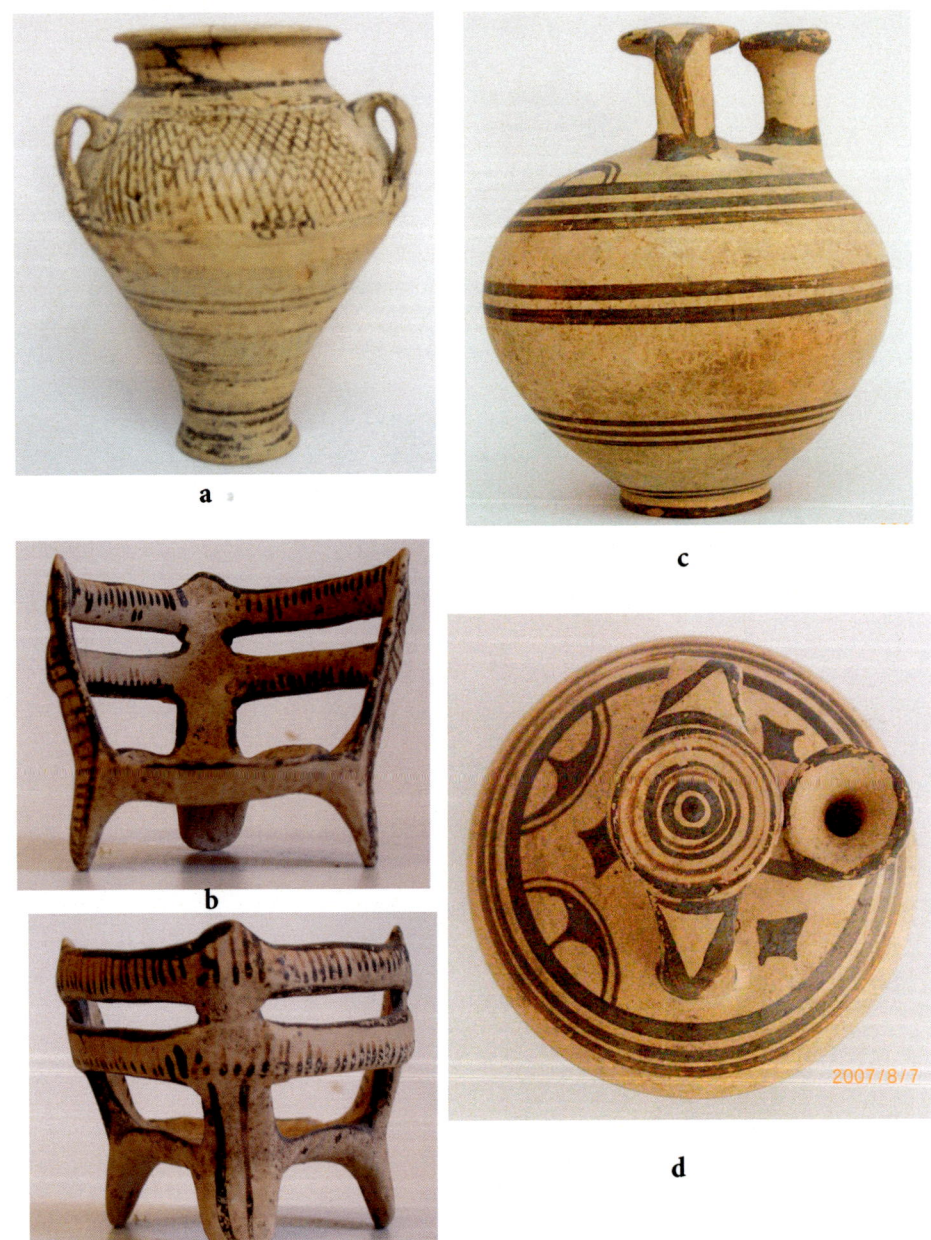

PLATE 6. PIRIFORM JAR NO. 397; THRONE NO. 386; STIRRUP JAR NO. 387.

PLATES AND FIGURES 67

PLATE 7. STIRRUP JAR NO. 569; JUG NO. 493; JUG NO. 495; SHERDS OF A LARGE JAR NO. 496; LEKYTHOS NO. 387.

PLATE 8. BASELESS ASKOS NO. 383; ROUNDED ALABASTRON NO. 384; STIRRUP JAR NO. 385; STIRRUP JAR NO. 389.

PLATE 9. STIRRUP JARS NOS. 390, 391; JUG NO. 392.

70   Excavations at the Mycenaean Cemetery at Aigion – 1967

a   b

c   d

PLATE 10. SQUARE SIDED ALABASTRA NOS. 393, 394; JUG NO. 475; AMPHORISKOS NO. 476.

PLATES AND FIGURES 71

a

b

c

d

PLATE 11. STIRRUP JARS NOS. 477, 479; JUG NO. 478.

PLATE 12. STIRRUP JARS NOS. 480, 399, 400; AMPHORISKOS NO. 398.

a

b

c

d

PLATE 13. ROUNDED ALABASTRON NO. 401; STRAIGHT-SIDED ALABASTRON NO. 402; KYLIX NO. 418.

a

b

c

d

PLATE 14. *AMPHORISKOI NOS. 419, 420, 421; STRAIGHT-SIDED ALABASTRON NO. 422.*

PLATES AND FIGURES   75

a

b

c

d

PLATE 15. JUG NO. 425; AMPHORISKOS NO. 426; STRAIGHT-SIDED ALABASTON NO. 427, BASED STRAIGHT-SIDED ALABASTRON NO. 428.

a b

c d

PLATE 16. BASED ASKOS NO. 429; STIRRUP JARS NOS. 430, 431.

PLATES AND FIGURES   77

a

b

c

d

PLATE 17. STIRRUP JAR NO. 432; AMPHORISKOI NOS. 433, 434.

78   Excavations at the Mycenaean Cemetery at Aigion – 1967

a   b

c   d

Plate 18. Amphoriskos No. 435; stirrup jars Nos. 436, 437.

PLATE 19. STIRRUP JARS NOS. 438, 439, 440, 441.

PLATE 20. STIRRUP JAR NO. 443; BASED ASKOS NO. 488.

a

b

c

d

PLATE 21. STIRRUP JAR NO. 489; ROUNDED ALABASTRA NOS. 444, 552.

ab

cd

PLATE 22. SHALLOW CUP NO. 553; KYLIX NO. 564; STIRRUP JAR NO. 565.

a

b

c　　　　　　　　　　d

Plate 23. Stirrup jars Nos. 566, 567, 568.

a

b

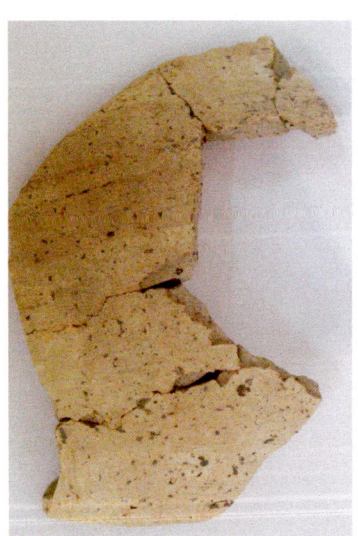

c

PLATE 24. POTTERY SHERDS NOS. 100, 104, 110, 101, 102.

PLATE 25. POTTERY SHERDS NOS. 103, 106, 107, 108, 109, 111.

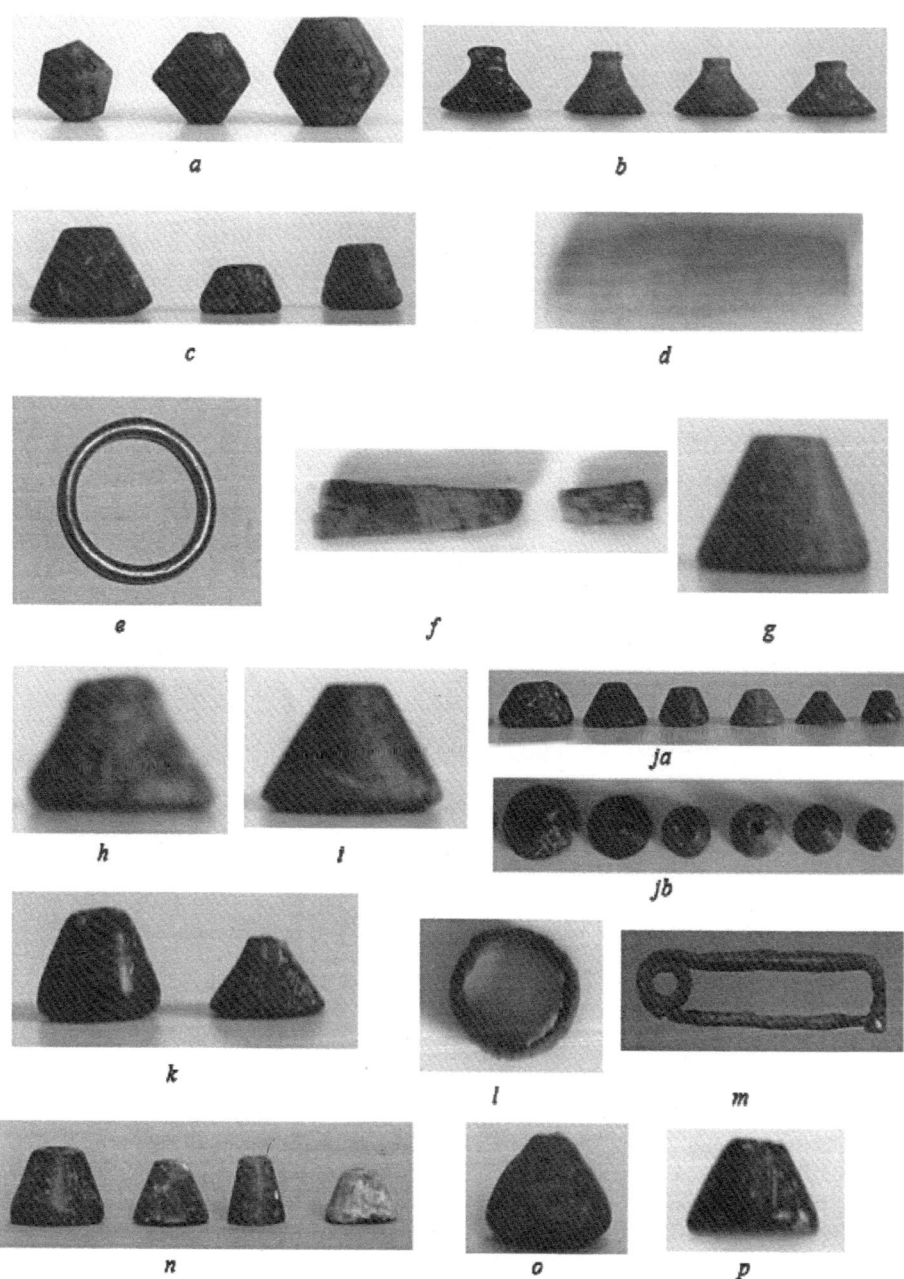

PLATE 26. ARTEFACTS.

FIGURE 1. STIRRUP JARS NOS. 414, 415.

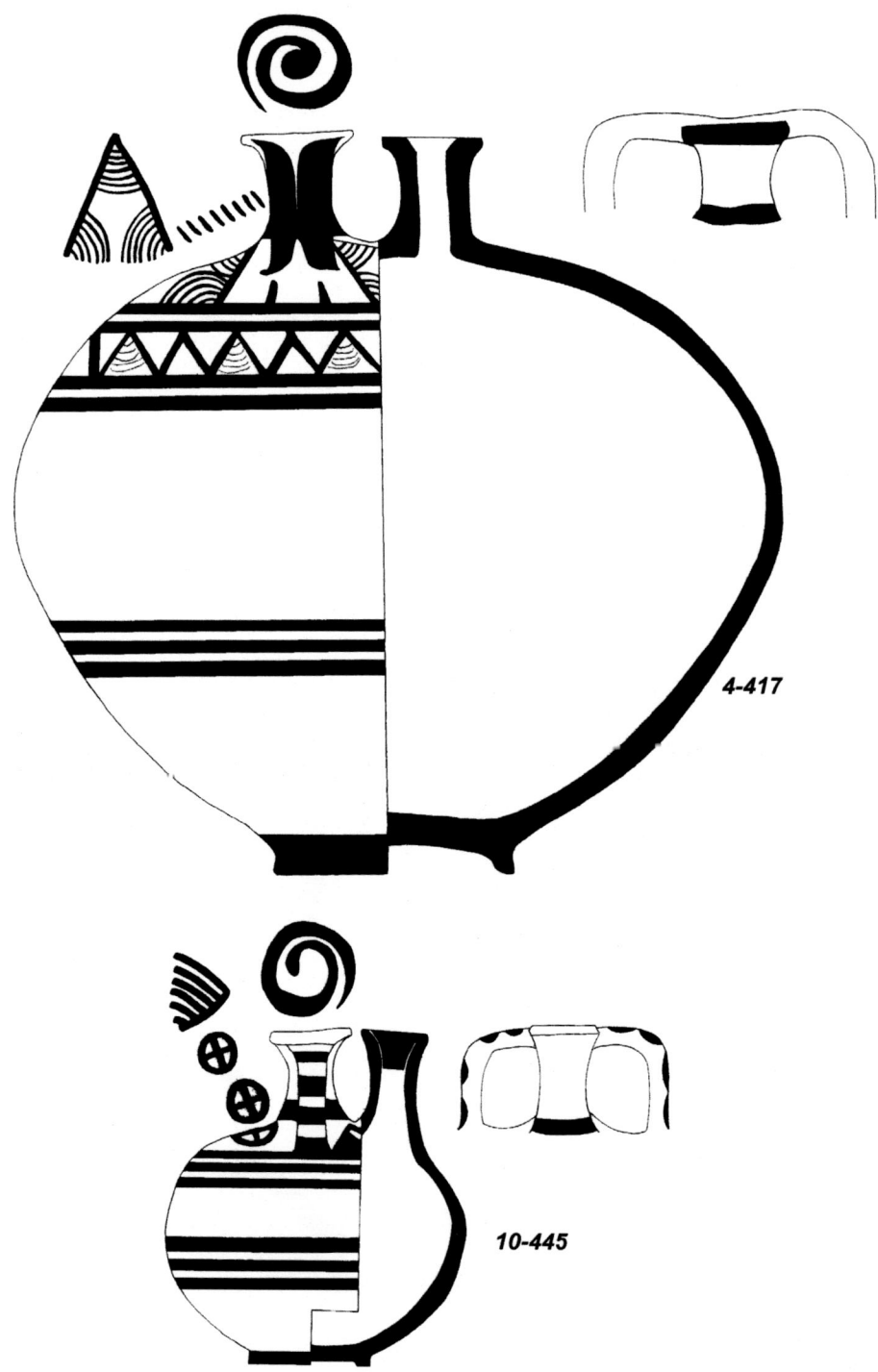

FIGURE 2. STIRRUP JARS NOS. 417, 445.

FIGURE 3. STIRRUP JARS NOS. 446, 447.

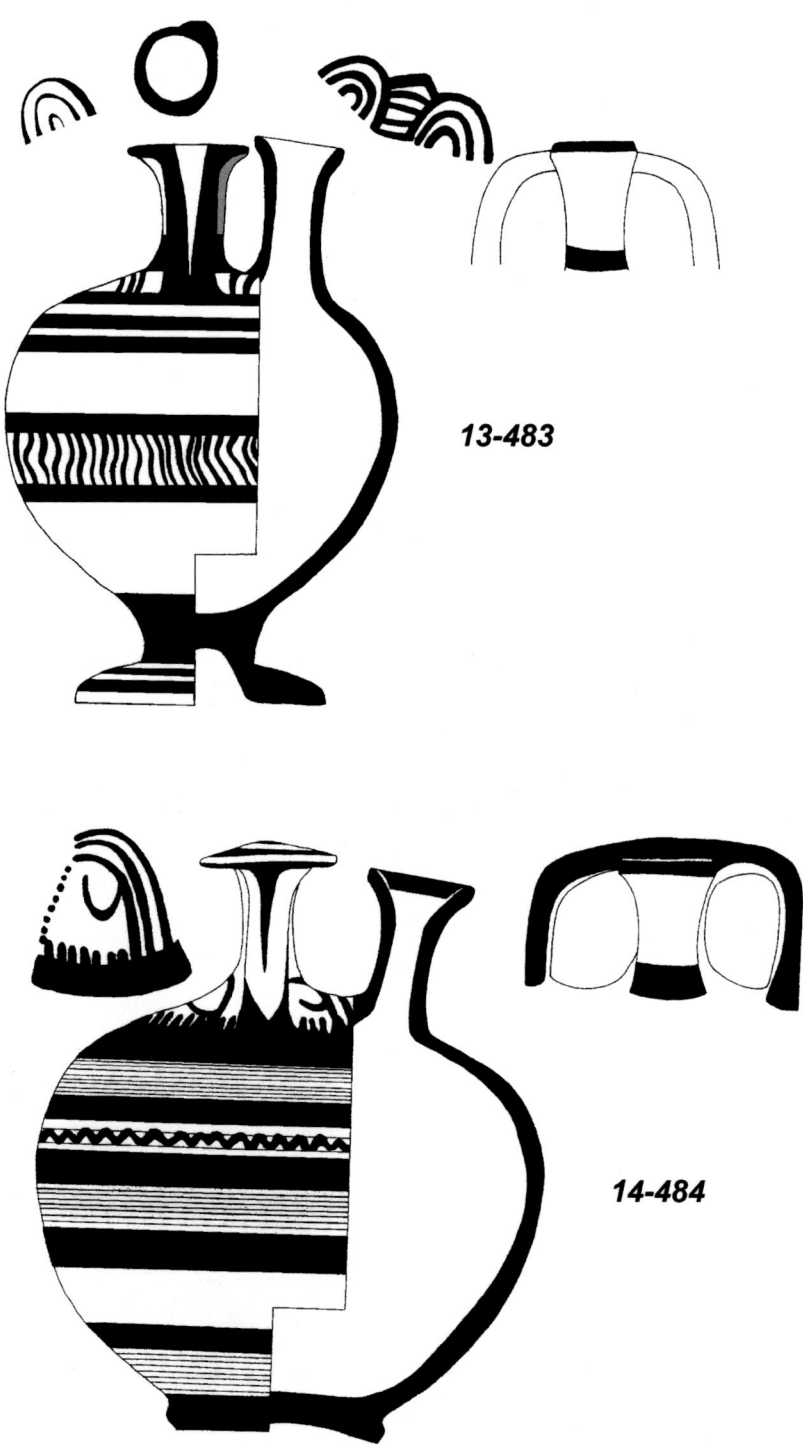

FIGURE 4. STIRRUP JARS NOS. 483, 484.

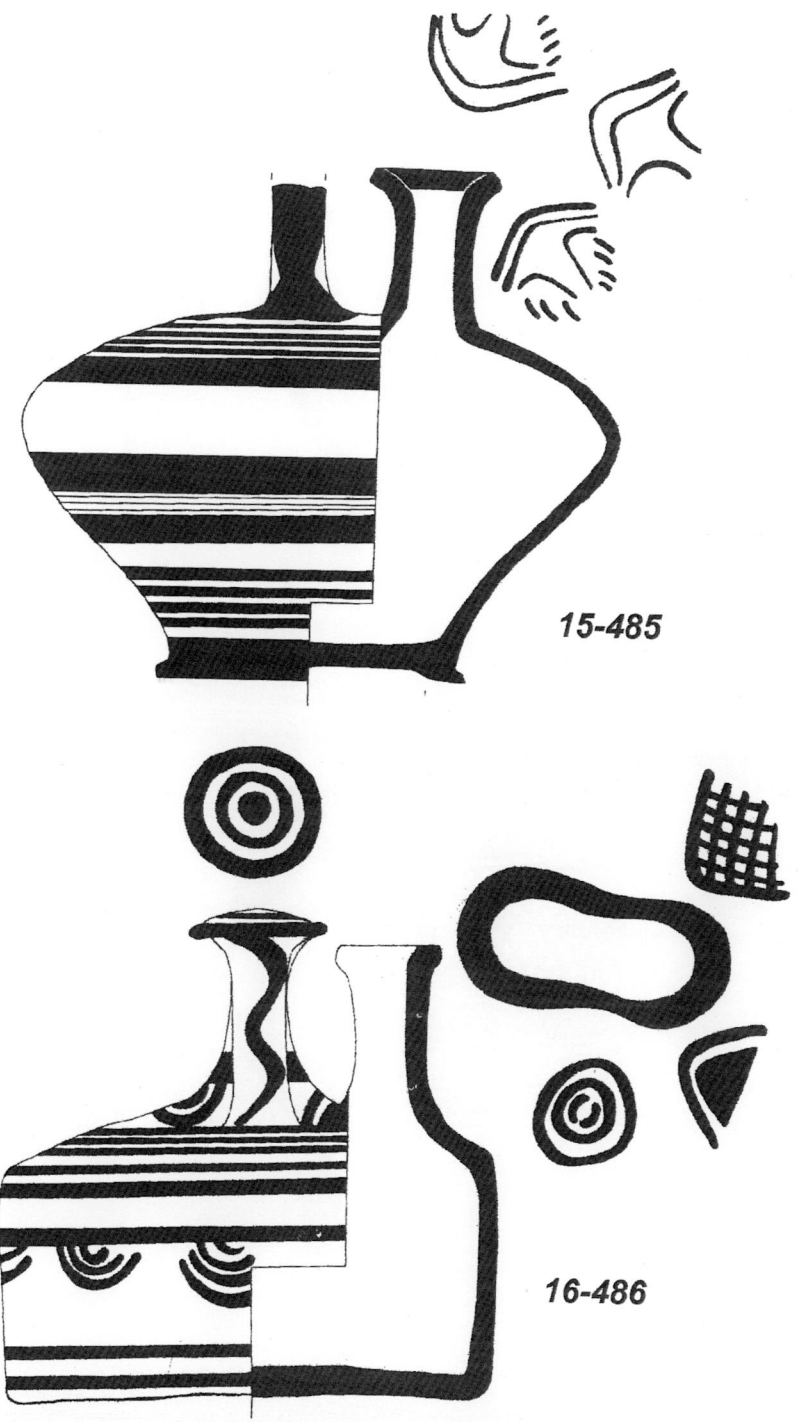

FIGURE 5. STIRRUP JARS NOS. 485, 486.

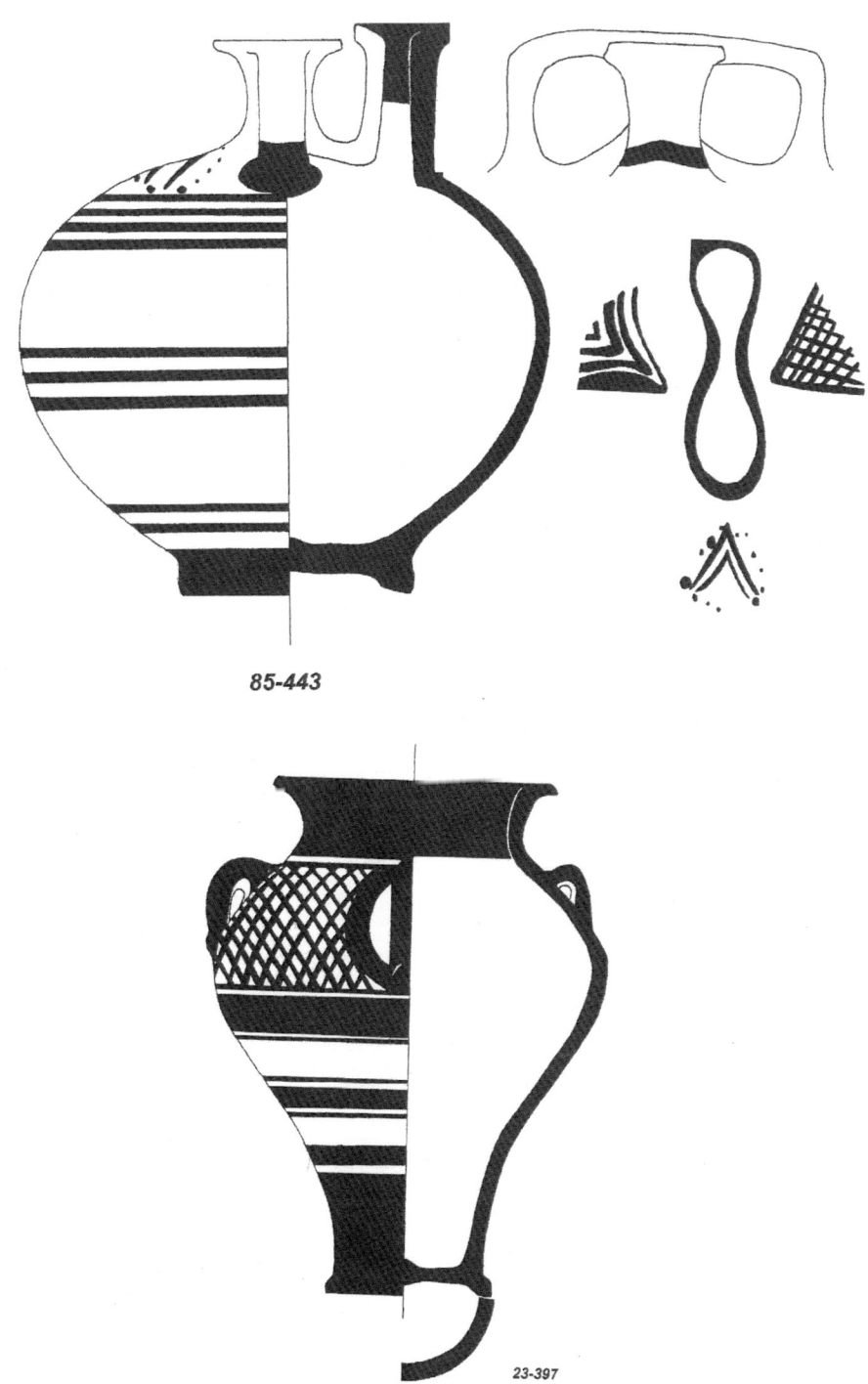

FIGURE 6. STIRRUP JAR NO. 443; PIRIFORM JAR NO. 397.

PLATES AND FIGURES   93

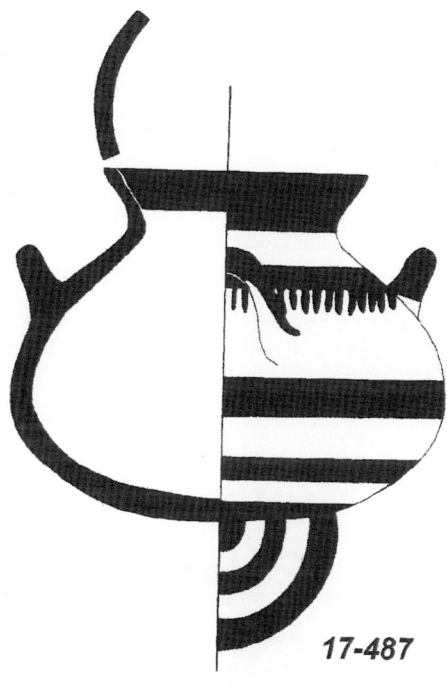

17-487

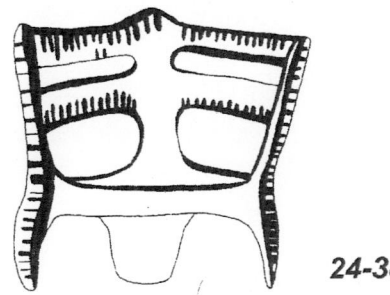  

24-386

FIGURE 7. ROUNDED ALABASTRON NO. 487; THRONE NO. 386.

94　Excavations at the Mycenaean Cemetery at Aigion – 1967

Figure 8. Stirrup jars Nos. 391, 387.

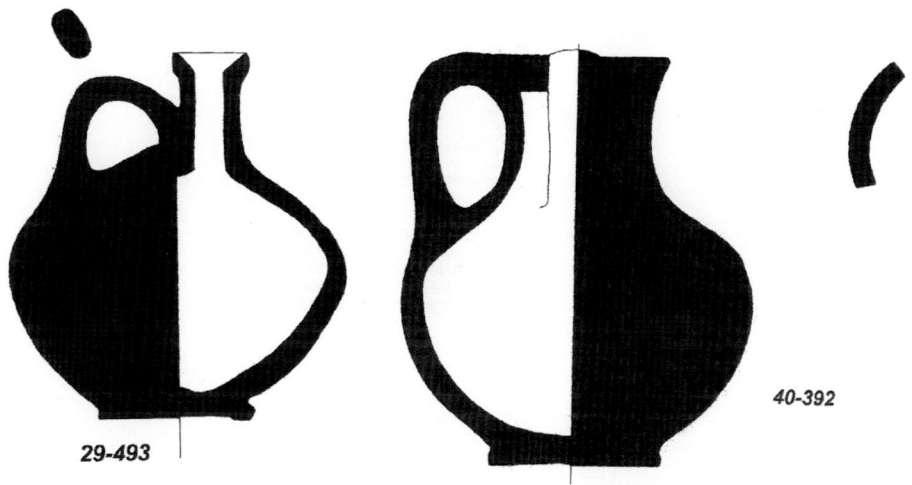

FIGURE 9. LEKYTHOS NO. 493; JUG NO. 392; STIRRUP JAR NO. 385.

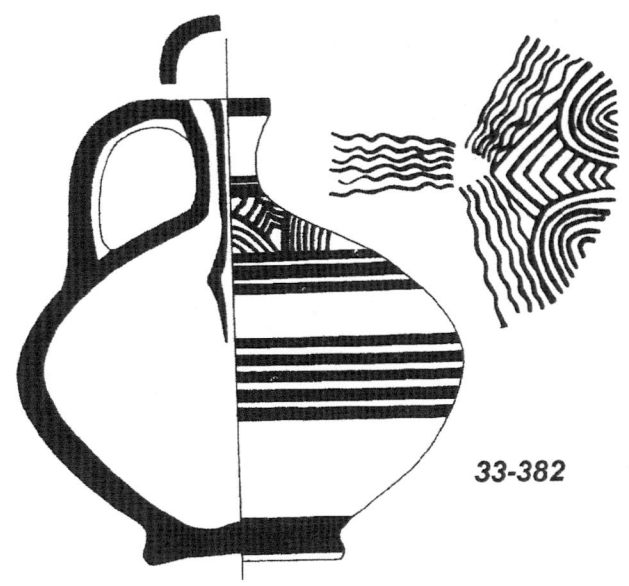

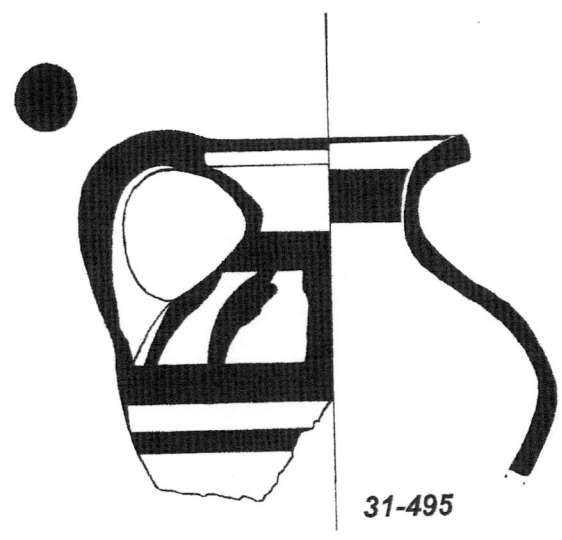

FIGURE 10. LEKYTHOS NO. 382; JUG NO. 495

PLATES AND FIGURES 97

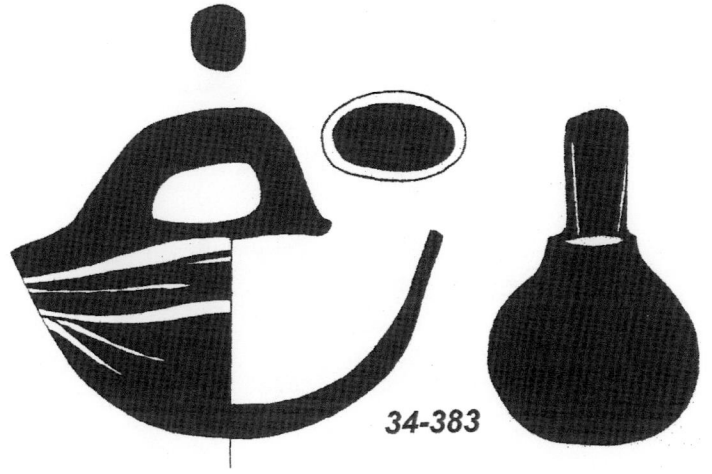

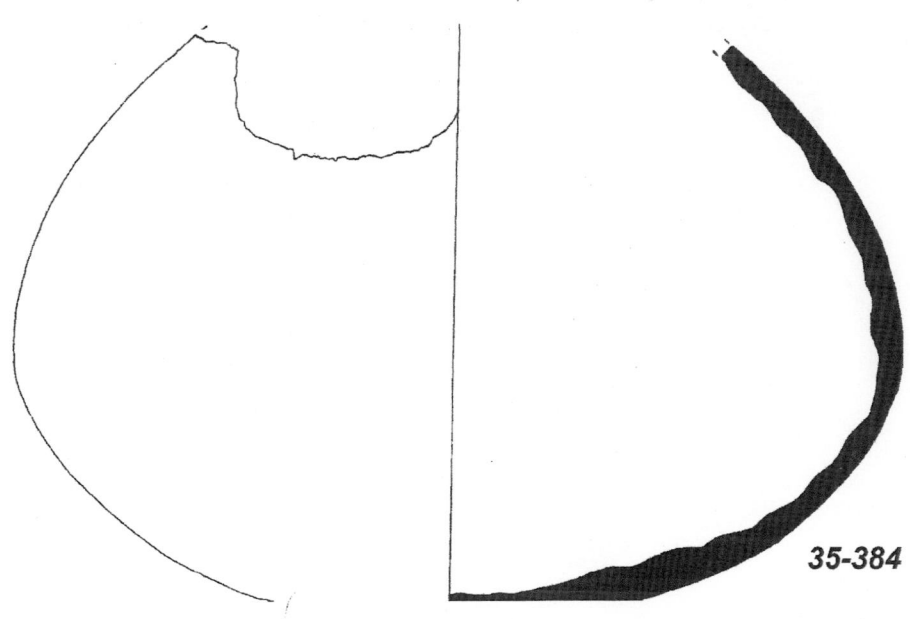

FIGURE 11. BASELESS ASKOS NO. 383; ROUNDED ALABASTRON 384.

FIGURE 12. STIRRUP JARS/JUGS NOS. 479, 389.

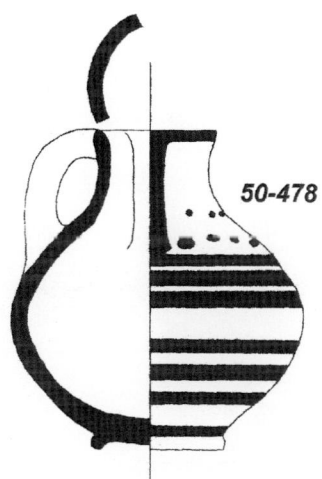

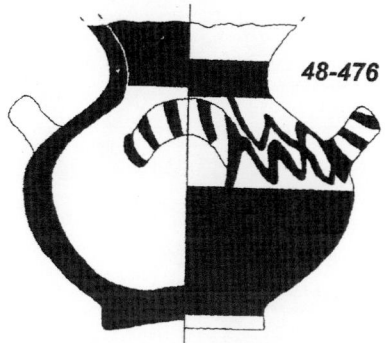

FIGURE 13. JUGS NOS. 475, 478; AMPHORISKOS NO. 476.

FIGURE 14. NOS 480, 399

PLATES AND FIGURES 101

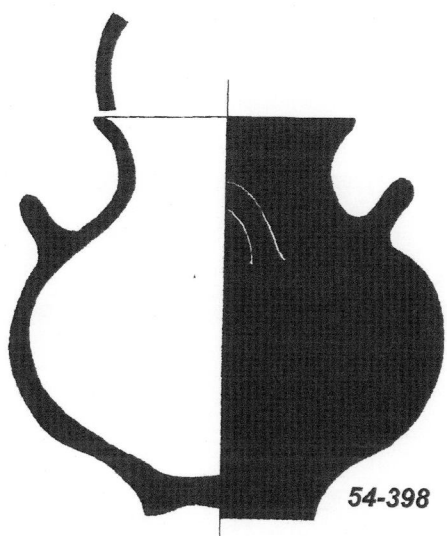

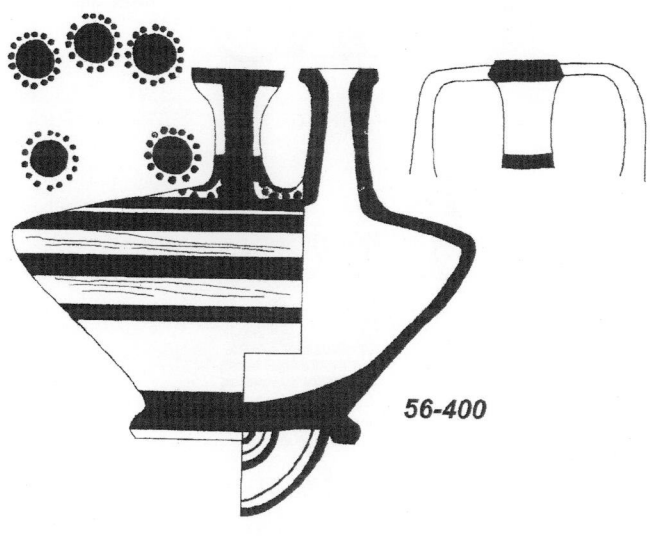

FIGURE 15. AMPHORISKOS NO. 398; STIRRUP JAR NO. 400.

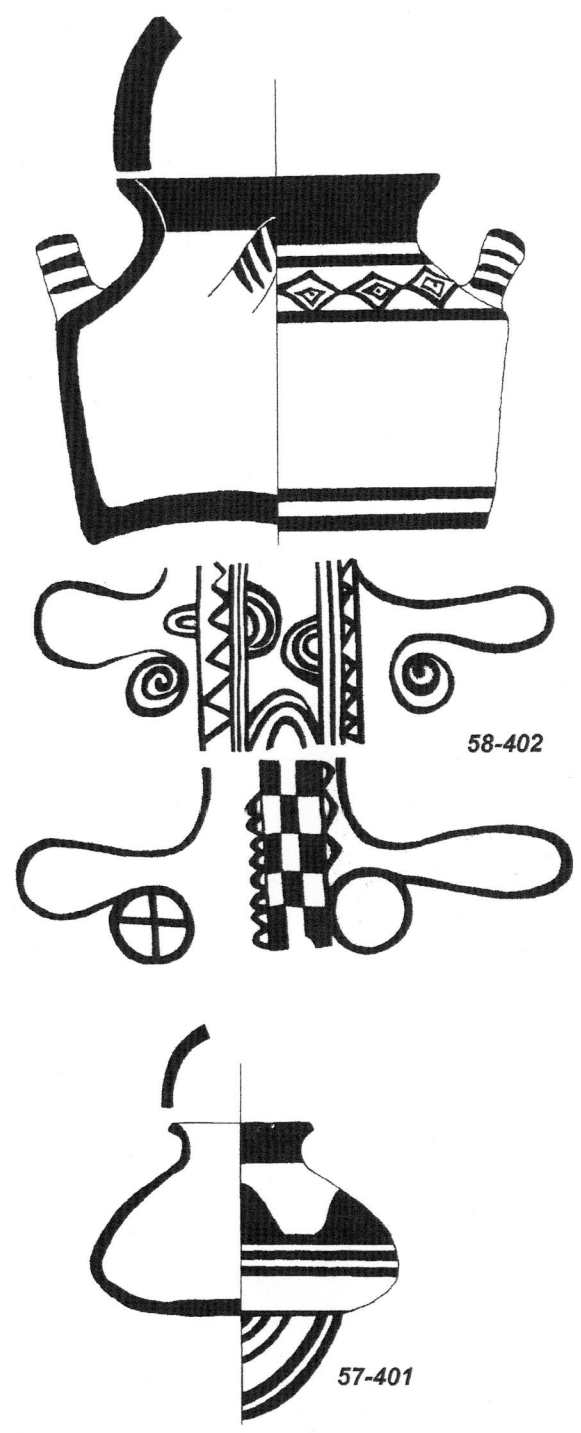

FIGURE 16. STRAIGHT SIDED ALABASTRON NO. 402; ROUNDED ALABASTRON NO. 401.

PLATES AND FIGURES 103

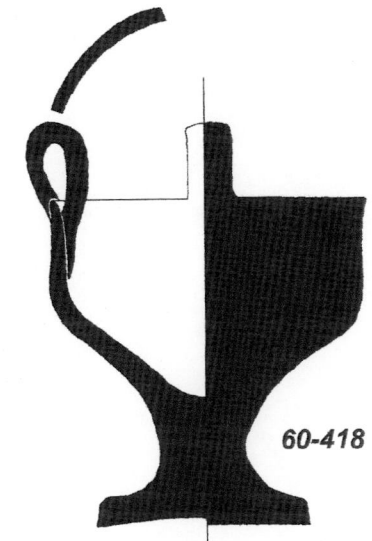

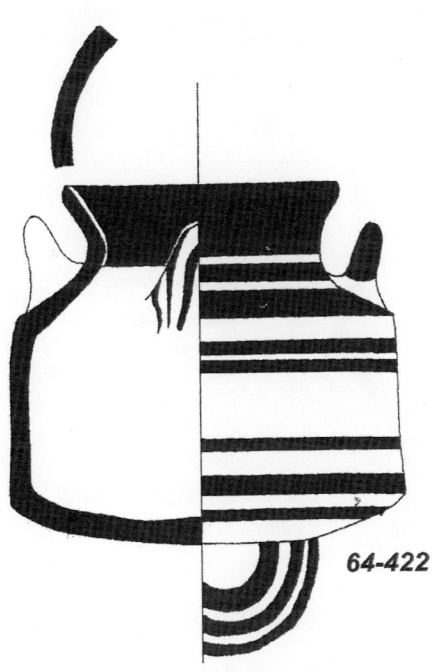

FIGURE 17. KYLIX 418, STRAIGHT SIDED ALABASTRON 422

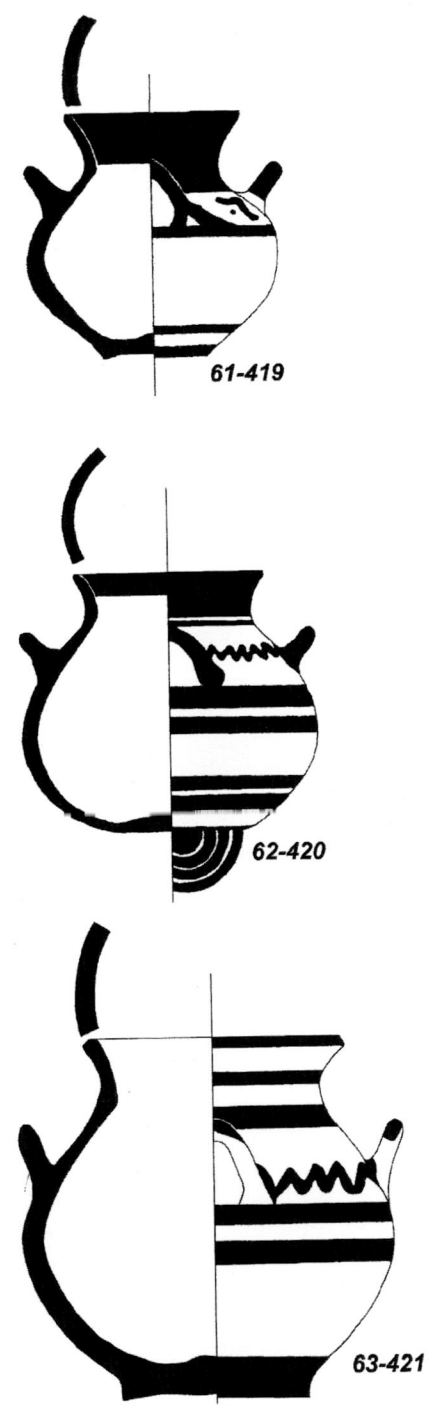

FIGURE 18. AMPHORISKOI NOS. 419, 420, 421.

PLATES AND FIGURES 105

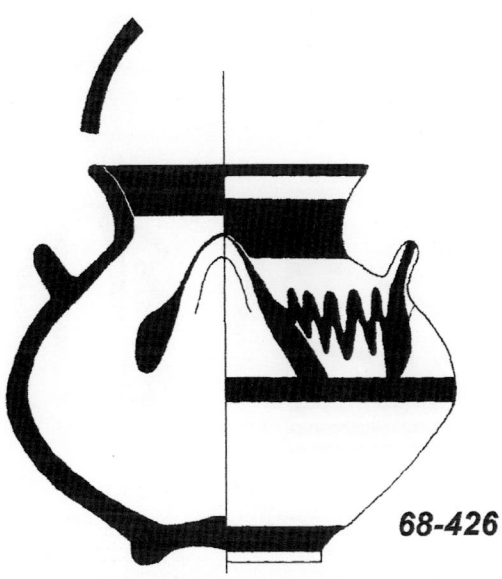

Figure 19. Jug No. 425; Amphoriskos No. 426.

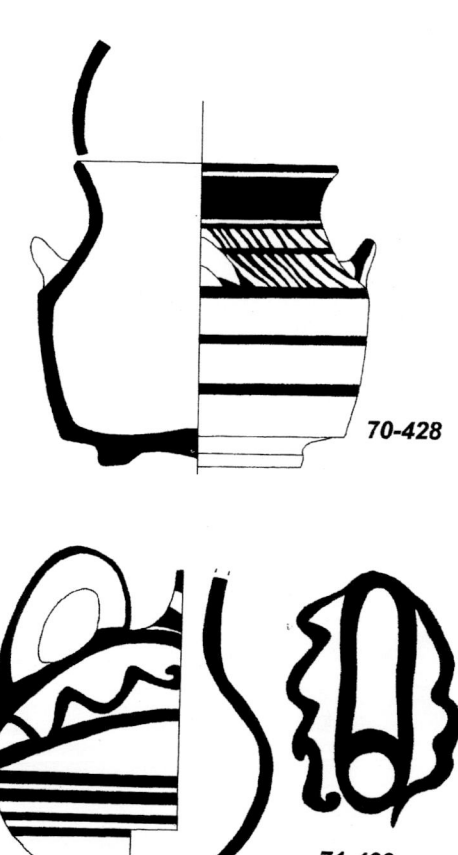

FIGURE 20. STRAIGHT SIDED ALABASTRA NOS. 427, 428; BASED ASKOS NO. 429.

PLATES AND FIGURES 107

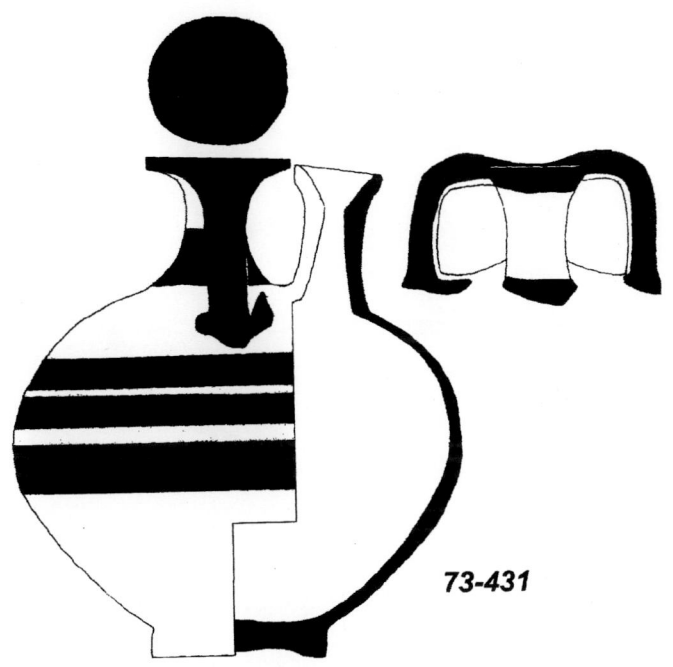

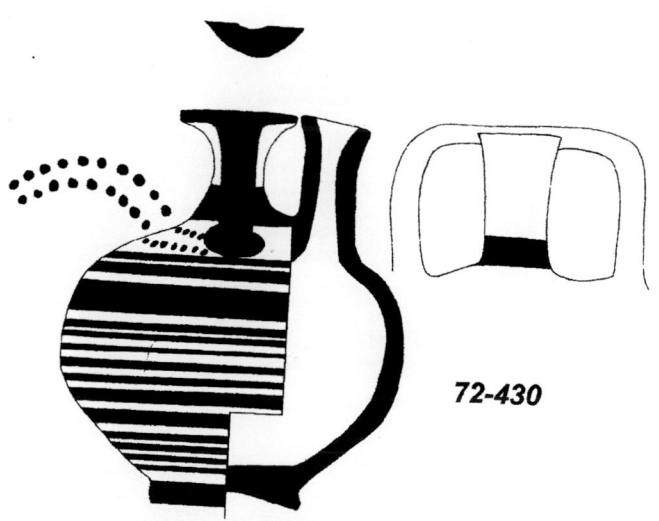

FIGURE 21. STIRRUP JARS NOS. 431, 430.

108 EXCAVATIONS AT THE MYCENAEAN CEMETERY AT AIGION – 1967

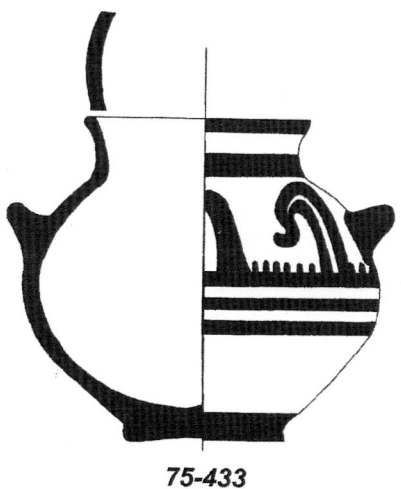

FIGURE 22. STIRRUP JAR NO. 432; AMPHORISKOS NO. 433.

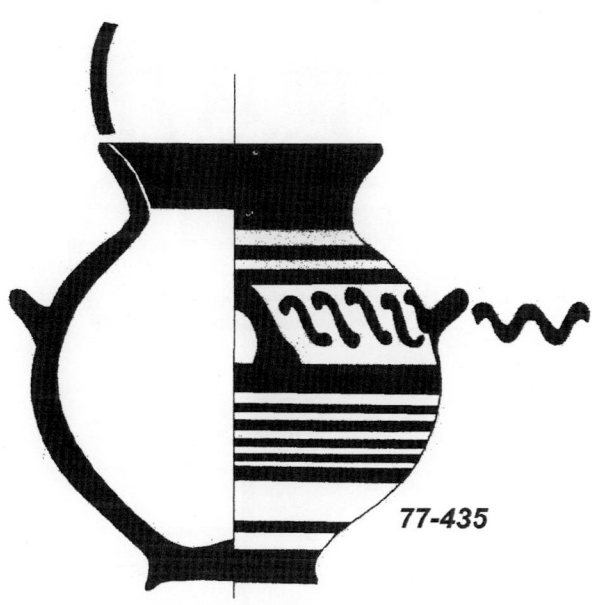

FIGURE 23. AMPHORISKOI NOS. 434, 435.

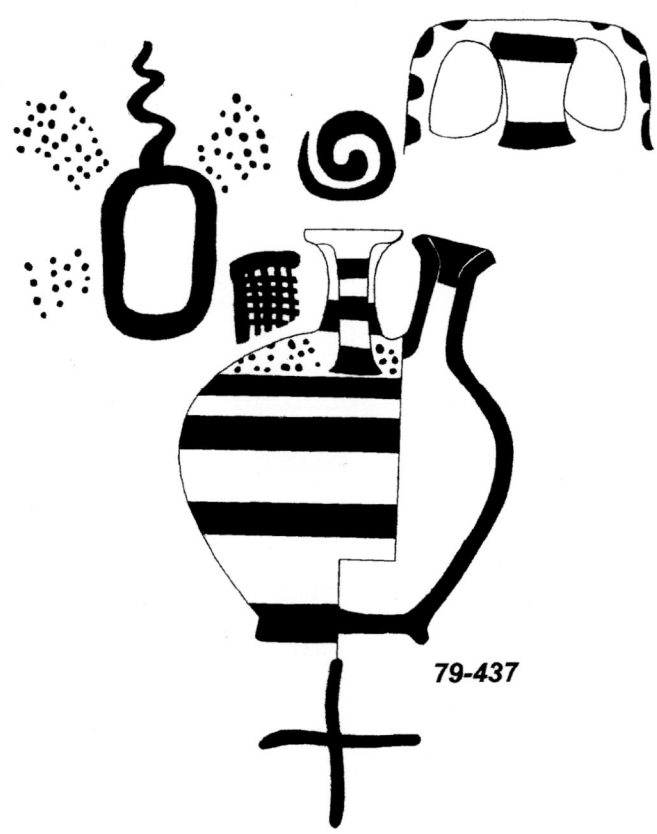

FIGURE 24. STIRRUP JARS NOS. 436, 437.

PLATES AND FIGURES 111

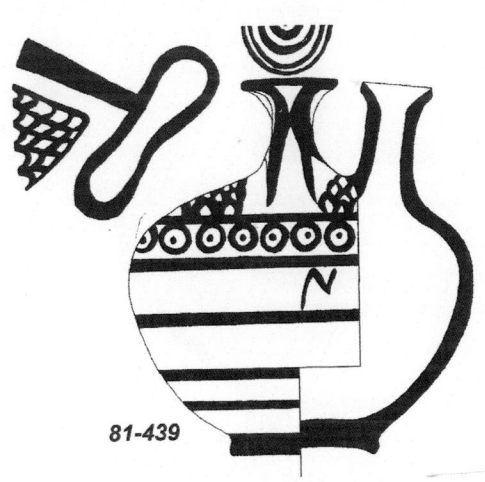

FIGURE 25. STIRRUP JARS NOS. 438, 439.

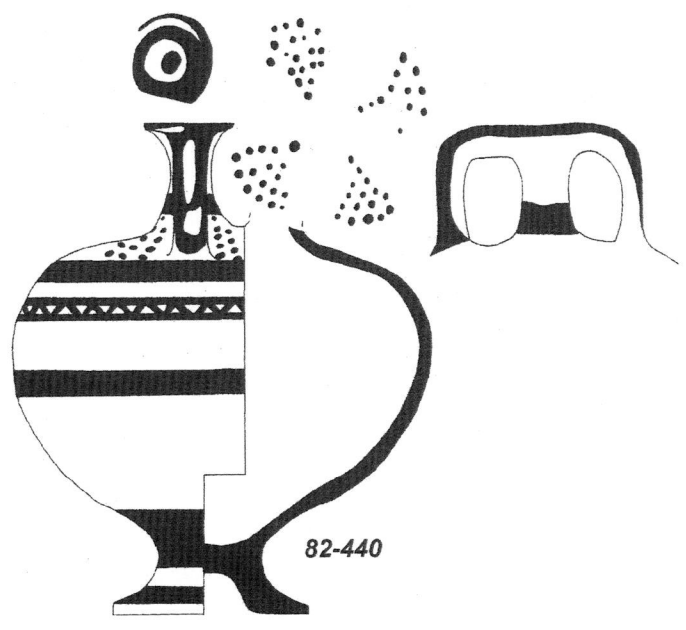

FIGURE 26. STIRRUP JARS NOS. 440, 441.

PLATES AND FIGURES 113

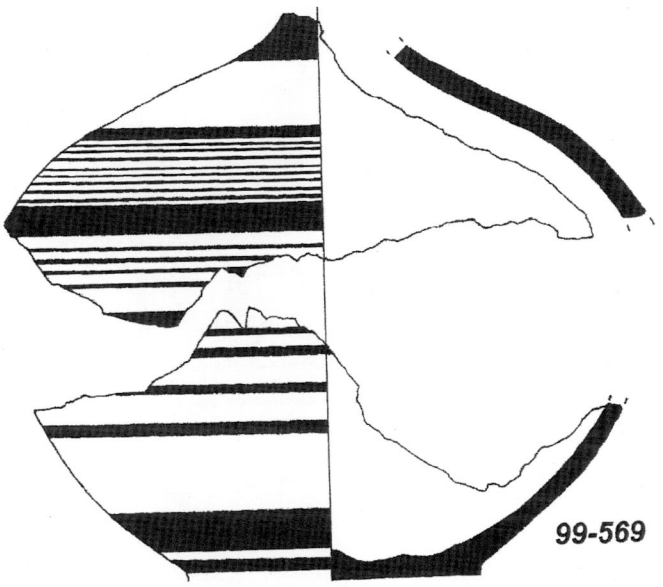

99-569

86-444

FIGURE 27. STIRRUP JAR 569, ROUNDED ALABASTRON NO. 444.

114 Excavations at the Mycenaean Cemetery at Aigion – 1967

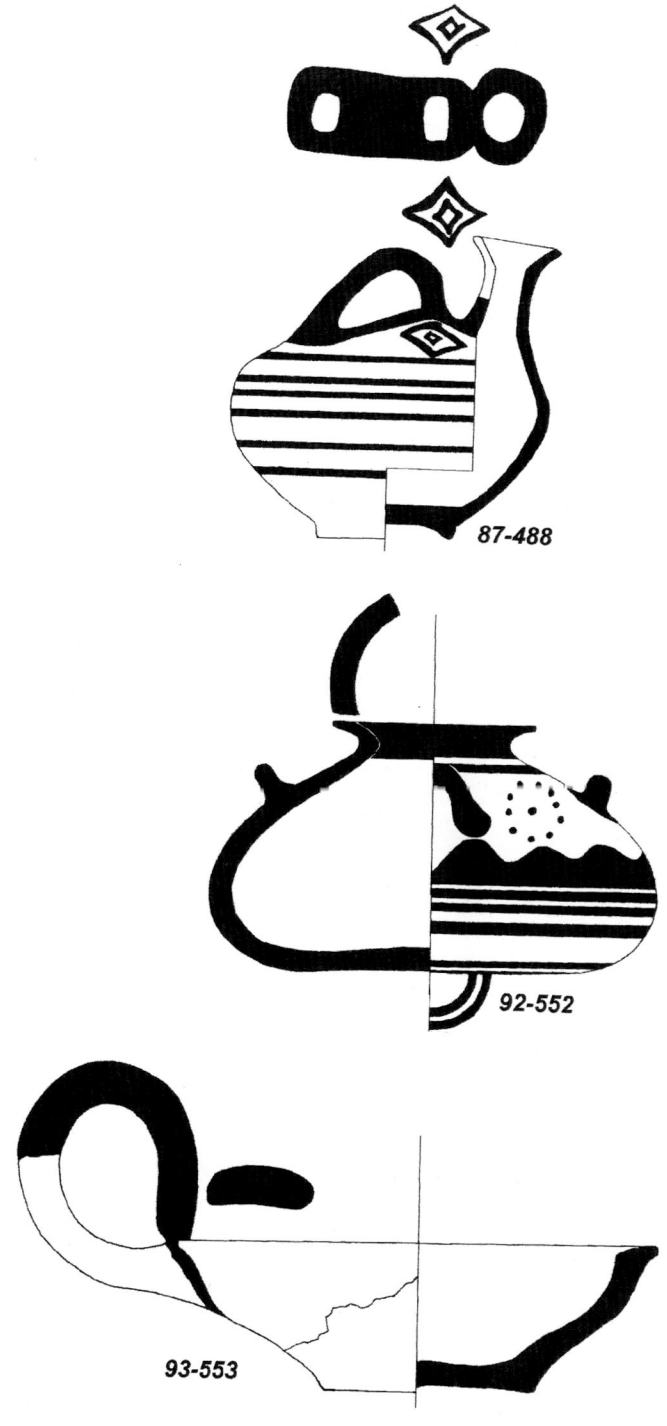

Figure 28. Based askos 488, rounded alabastron 552, shallow cup 553

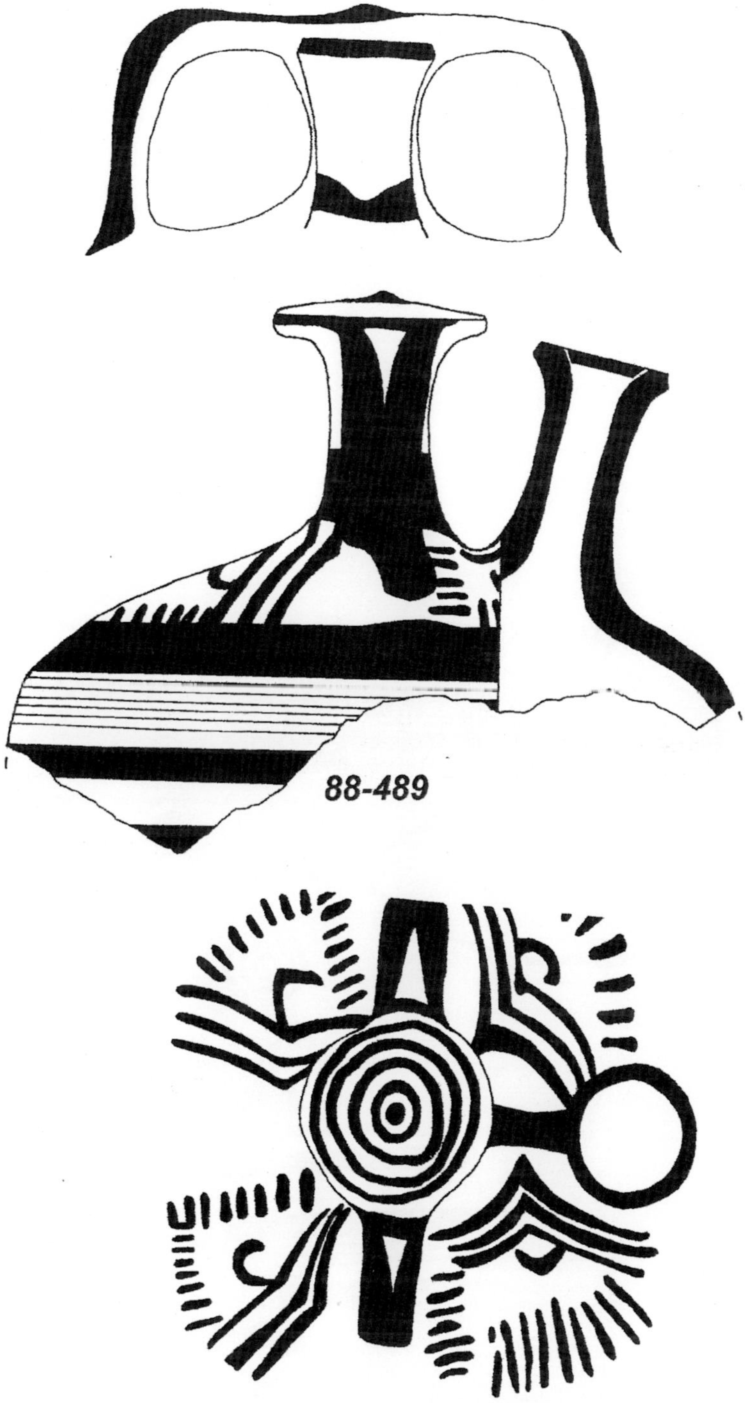

FIGURE 29. STIRRUP JAR NO. 489.

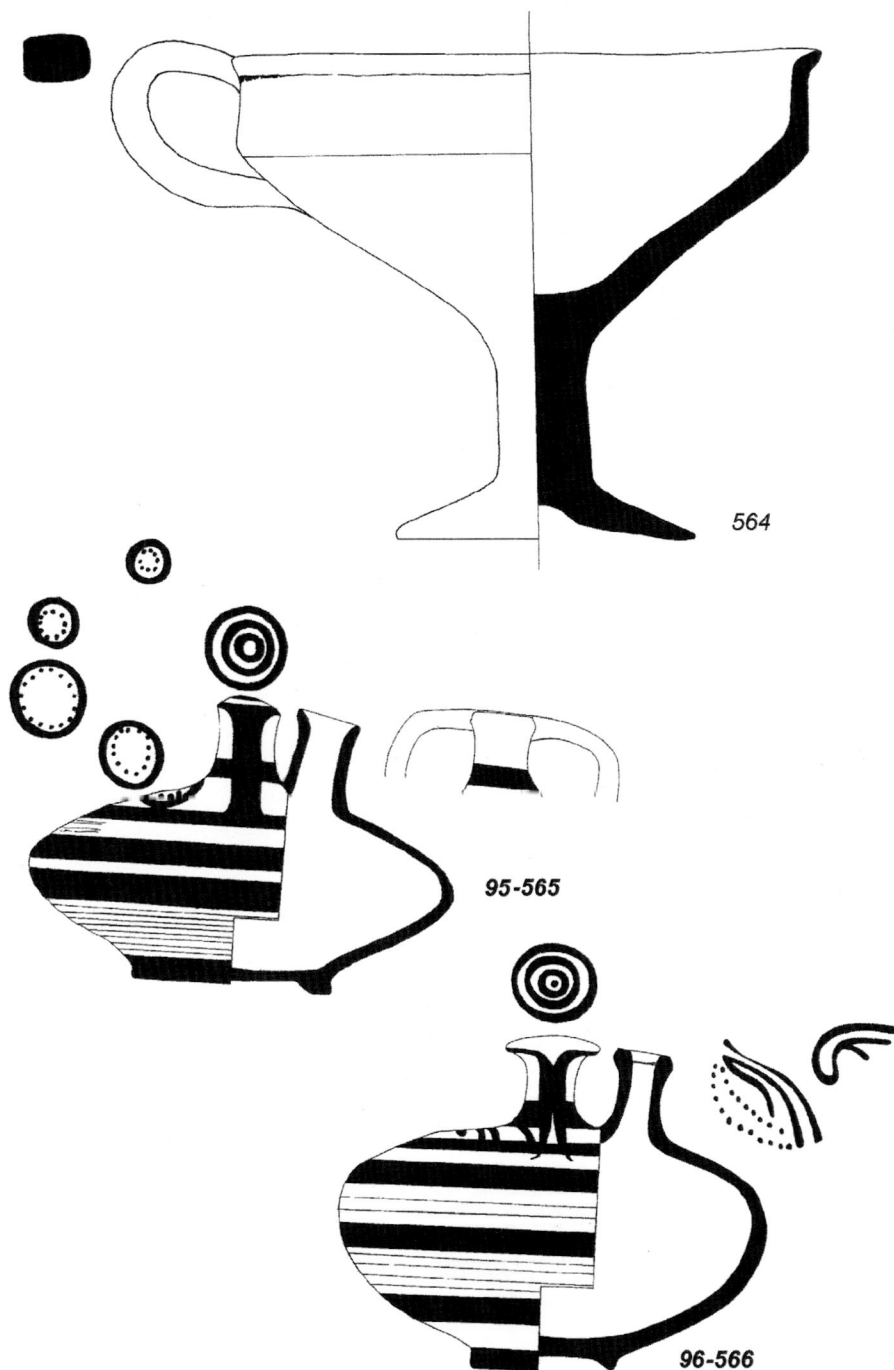

FIGURE 30. CARINATED KYLIX 564, STIRRUP JARS 565,566

FIGURE 31. STIRRUP JARS NOS. 567, 568, 100 (?).

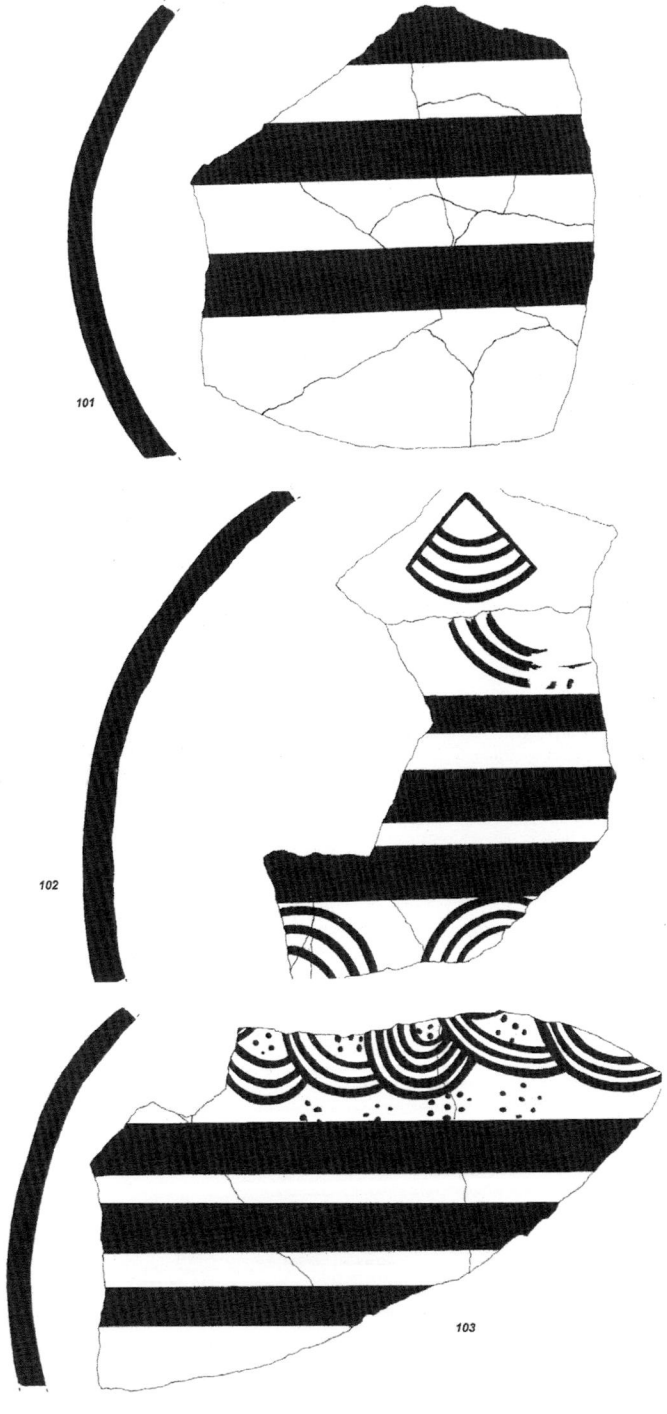

FIGURE 32. SHERDS OF LARGE PIRIFORM JARS NOS. 101, 102, 103.

PLATES AND FIGURES 119

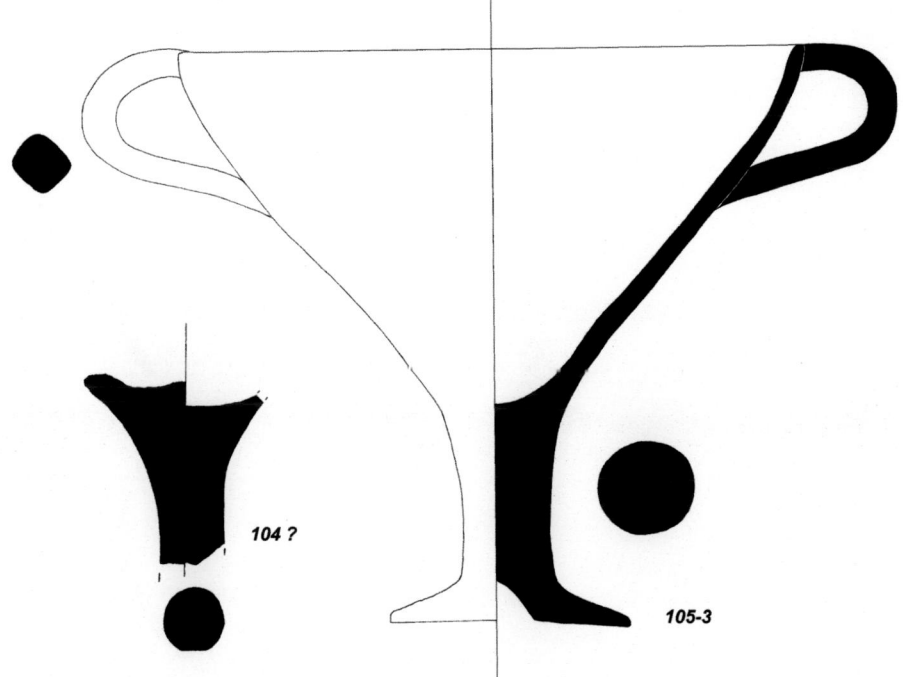

FIGURE 33. KYLIKES NOS. 104, 105.

FIGURE 34. FRAGMENTS OF KYLIX NO. 106, BOWL OR SHALLOW CUP NO. 107 AND BOWL OR SPOUTED CUP NO. 108.

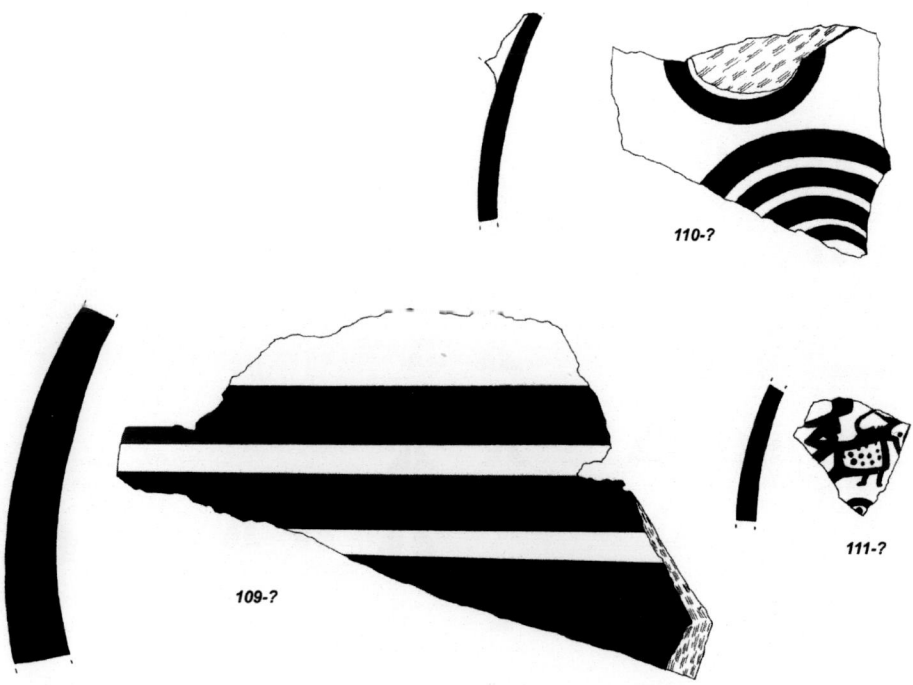

FIGURE 35. FRAGMENTS OF LARGE PIRIFORM JARS NOS. 109, 110, AND PICTORIAL VASE NO. 111.

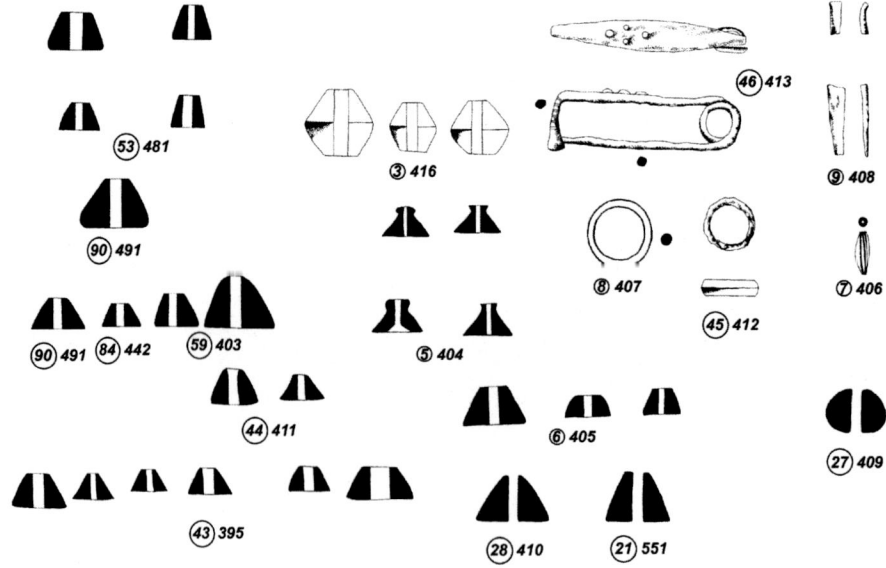

FIGURE 36. ARTEFACTS.